Publisher's Note

The book descriptions we ask booksellers to display prominently warn that this is an historic book with numerous typos or missing text; it is not indexed or illustrated.

The book was created using optical character recognition software. The software is 99 percent accurate if the book is in good condition. However, we do understand that even one percent can be an annoying number of typos! And sometimes all or part of a page may be missing from our copy of the book. Or the paper may be so discolored from age that it is difficult to read. We apologize and gratefully acknowledge Google's assistance.

After we re-typeset and design a book, the page numbers change so the old index and table of contents no longer work. Therefore, we often remove them; otherwise, please ignore them.

We carefully proof read any book that will sell enough copies to cover the cost of proof reading. Unfortunately, we couldn't afford to proof read this book. Sorry. Instead we try to let customers download a free copy of the original typo-free scanned book. Simply enter the barcode number from the back cover of the paperback in the Free Book form at www.RareBooksClub.com. You may also qualify for a free trial membership in our book club to download up to four books for free. Simply enter the barcode number from the back cover onto the membership form on our home page. The book club entitles you to select from more than a million books at no additional charge. Simply enter the title or subject onto the search form to find the books.

If you have any questions, could you please be so kind as to consult our Frequently Asked Questions page at www.RareBooksClub.com/faqs.cfm? You are also welcome to contact us there.

General Books LLC™, Memphis, USA, 2012. ISBN: 9781150620348.

⚘ ⚘ ⚘ ⚘ ⚘ ⚘ ⚘ ⚘

THE BOY, SOME HORSES, AND A GIRL
THE BOY, SOME HORSES,
AND A GIRL
H Ttale of an 3risb TErfp
DOROTHEA CONYERS.'
i
Author Of 'Peter's Pedigree'
ELEVENTH IMPRESSION
LONDON
EDWARD ARNOLD
41 & 43 MADDOX STREET. BOND STREET. W.
1905
Aii rifhti racratd
THE NEW YORK PUBLIC LIBEABT ASTOR, LENOX AND TILDEfl FOUNDATIONS
B ii)51 L CONTENTS

THE BOY, SOME HORSES,
AND A GIRL
V CHAPTER I HOW THE TRIP CAME TO BE TALKED OF

Twilight was closing in. All day the woodlands had echoed to the sound of the guns. The slaughter of the innocents, carefully reared that they might be thus slaughtered, had begun, and long lines of little brown bodies had been laid on the grass.

Evenings were chilly; a wood fire hissed and crackled cheerfully while three men, standing at an open French window, looked back at it, applauding its energy, and resolving that in a moment—when they had acquired a comfortable chill—they would go and sit over its noisy warmth.

'It's a sin. A shame!' Fitzroy Travers waved a stumpy pipe with oratorical energy. 'A ripping place to shoot in, but winter's coming. We're getting into October (September never lasts long), and look at the place—plough, plough, varied by woods. Bah!'

The others followed the line of his expressive pipe. Slope upon slope of cultured land; billowing hills with great woods clinging to their sides as far as the eye could reach; brown plough and yellowing stubble—a prosperous country, but, of a truth, not one to hunt a fox in.

'If one could find a trained elephant!' said Kane-Norton, with the air of one who has compassed something witty.

'Try a fresh one, Nor,' growled Travers sourly; the landscape was shortening his temper. 'Eh, it's sickening; the best hunter in England in the stables, and—and what can she do here?'

At this stage the Boy chimed in. They called him the Boy because he had once been one. The others were men of about thirtyfive, and a gulf of ten years stretched between them and Norman Rivers; so the Boy he remained. He was rubbing up his gun tenderly, and spoke with a bit of oily rag between his teeth:

'Why don't you try Ireland?' he asked.

'I've often thought of it,' said Travers, but without any enthusiasm in his voice.

'Thinking's no use—no use at all.'

The Boy dropped the rag, and pulled

a letter out of his pocket.

'This put it into my head,' he said. A cousin of mine has just gone to Cahirvally with his regiment, and he says it's a place to dream of.'

He opened the letter.

'H'm! Now I've got it! "So here we are, waiting for the winter, in such a country! Nothing but grass and grass, and grass beyond that again!"'

Here Travers remarked that he thought the country must have been specially laid out for Nebuchadnezzar.

'Shut up!' said the Boy, reading on. '" Stone walls and banks to jump. Bless you, the people only live to hunt! We're cubbing now. The town's wretched, everyone poor as rats. You don't see a decent turn-out in the place; the houses all want plaster, some of them roofs; but the owners have got horses— *with* a capital H. I tell you I'm looking forward to my winters here: three days a week—just enough for a poor subaltern with a limited stud, with heaps of indifferent shooting to keep one occupied in between. If I were you fellows, I'd come here, instead of tilling the land for them in Essex. Horses are for nothing. You only pay about sixty for a beast which would cost you double in England. Most of the fellows seem to live by coping. Hay and corn, too, after the English prices, are good things for the poor."'

The Boy shut up the letter. 'Sounds fine, don't it?' he said.

The other two let their eyes light and their pipes go out. It was all very well to scoff about Nebuchadnezzar, but—' grass and grass, and grass again.' They looked at the brown wooded landscape, dim now in the twilight, and swore softly.

'I'm fairly well off, too, this year,' observed Kane-Norton. 'But it costs such a fortune moving, and the shires are quite beyond us.'

The Boy had only begun to hunt a year ago; it was now the dream of his life.

'I've got my old aunt's legacy,' he cried. 'It would do a winter's hunting. Who knows? *I* might do well, and make my exes on the horses. Oh, I say, you

two, come to Ireland I Buy hunters cheap; sell 'em dear again over here. Oh, let's do it—let's do it Have our season for nothing, and quit this turned-up land.'

'But what about the horses going wrong?" mildly queried the man who knew horse-flesh.

'They can't all go wrong,' said the Boy.

'But you can't even ride yet,' observed KaneNorton.

'I'm learning,' said the Boy cheerfully. 'I had three falls off the Norma filly this morning. One must only go on until one can do the thing. Come to Cahirvally.'

'Your cousin appears to be enthusiastic. Is he an Irishman?' Travers asked.

'Half-bred, as I am myself/ returned the Boy. 'It's his first visit there. Oh, I say, think of skimming over grass, instead of'

'Instead of being an impromptu human roller,' put in Kane-Norton unkindly.

'Just so,' said the Boy cheerily.

Travers and Kane-Norton, staid men, looked at each other thoughtfully. They were cousins, who would have been poor men apart, but by living together mustered a fair income. Travers supplied the house; which, unfortunately, was in the centre of the plough country, and houses cannot be moved. Its situation was a thorn in their soul, for they loved hunting.

This letter tempted them. Travers turned to look at the fire; then, a sign of mental perturbation, he thrust his pipe, still ablaze, into his pocket. 'Let's go to see the horses,' he said.

The Boy laid down his gun and chuckled softly.

The stables, warm brick buildings, stood at the back of the house, and Merrylass, by Merryman out of Bright Eyes, was being done over, standing up to her hocks in golden wheaten straw. Travers went in to look at her. She was a long, low bay, clean bred, and had cost him more money than he cared to think of; but the plough country killed her. She laboured hopelessly in its sticky depths. Travers liked pace, and grumbled at the

big, slow horses which the plough made a necessity. He looked at his favourite's sloping shoulders, and her powerful hocks, her galloping quarters. Given a chance, how she could fly! He stood staring.

Kane-Norton walked down the range of boxes; his stud were indisputable weight-carriers, and hardly the class of animal to fly across those distant pastures. Still, there was nothing which he was very much attached to, and his soul began to see green. 'Fitz, it's an inspiration. Let's go!' he called down the stable.

'I—I almost believe we will.' Travers ran a rapturous eye again over the mare. 'Think of her, you two, over those banks, her legs well under her. Jove! we'd show this Irishman what a horse can do.'

'I presume that settles it,' said the Boy meekly. He had no horse to look at, and hovered between the two.

Travers grunted scornfully. Already, in imagination, he was flying over grass fields, the pack in front, everyone else behind; and no insult could rouse him from his dream.

'Make up your mind to it, then,' said KaneNorton crisply. 'Cahirvally, then, in October. And—Heaven help you, Boy, if it doesn't pay us!'

James, Travers' stiff old groom, raised a listening head. Horror trickled down his stiff old back. 'Ireland, sir?' he queried. 'Take the horses to Ireland?'

'Yes,' said Travers, and the Boy's heart bounded. 'Good hunting there, James.'

Then, in measured tones—he had taught Travers to ride his first pony— old James declined to accompany them. 'I've been told, sir,' he said with emphasis, 'that in Ireland it's customary to be shot at from behind hedges and made corpses of'

Here the Boy remarked that the Land Bill had quite banished the corpses.

'And,' James went on, in his slow, distinct voice, 'that they eats nothing '—he found space here to wither the Boy with a look—' eats naught but potatoes and sleeps with the pigs; an' none of them things, Mister Fitzroy, would agree with a man of my years. I've met a few back from them parts, and, indeed, sir, it's no place to go, sir. Someone else must mind Merrylass, sir, in Ireland.'

The Boy, always unabashed, wondered whether they also would have to sleep with the pigs, or if it was an honour specially reserved for grooms.

It was the first damper, and James refused to alter his ultimatum. They could get them as was used to the ways, he said; he would stay and mind the young horses.

'Think of it, Fitz,' chuckled the Boy, as they went back to the house, leaving old James im placable. 'For the first time in your life you'll be able to ride the horse you want to.

'You be quiet, Boy,' retorted Travers; 'or we'll not disgrace England by taking you.'

The Boy grinned. He was a slim youth, with a peculiarly innocent expression, and sleepy blue eyes which contradicted the expression. He had been Travers' ward, and both KaneNorton and Travers, though they looked on him as a foolish youth, were extremely fond of him, passing over his sundry caustic remarks as a phase of his tender years.

When they got back to the house and the brightly blazing fire, the new idea did not die. They began to chatter of new saddles, of new coats, and, lastly, of new horses. Travers sunk in his big chair, a pipe in his mouth, had in his eye *exactly* the horse to cross an Irish country. He babbled, but his remarks were lost, because Kane-Norton from his side, his words slipping from the shelter of a mild cigar, was equally full of his ideals. The Boy sat in the middle, and strove—at first with some respect—to gather wisdom from their words. But at length he shook a bewildered and indignant head.

'Look here, y' know,' he broke in: 'I've been listening to you two chaps chattering like a pair of magpies because I'll want a horse or two myself. But if you must have horses well ribbed up to cross banks, why, then, breeding will carry you anywhere; and it doesn't matter a

rap about their shapes, yet they must have short backs, and if their hocks are right backs don't go for anything. You're like a pair of witches, you two, making charms, and here am I trying to gather up a grain of sense between you. If I took it all in, and bought accordingly, I tell you I'd have a funnylooking hunter.'

Travers and Kane-Nor ton woke from their speaking dream; neither had heard the other, but the Boy's voice broke the charm.

'Eh, what's that about buying?' they chorused. 'Look here, Boy: don't you go buying on your own, or goodness knows what kind of brute you'd pick up.'

'That's just what I've been wondering,' remarked the Boy.

'Well,' said Travers, 'you stop talking'—the Boy thought this was unnecessary—' and write to your cousin. Tell him to find us lodgings somewhere in Caliirvally. Don't let's think it over, or we might never start. We'll run over in October, pick up horses, and get to know the people before the regular hunting begins. I'm told the Irish people are extraordinary hospitable, and we shall have a rousing time.'

'Think of that grass,' murmured KaneNorton in dreamy ecstasy to the fire.

'And of Merrylass across those banks. Write, Boy,' said Travers.

'Hurrah!' said the Boy. 'Where's a pen and ink?'

So a letter had carried conviction to three minds; and if the three dreamt that night, it was of Nebuchadnezzar's country, stretching greenly to a background of dim purple hills. Field upon field of pasture; nothing to stop hounds or horses.

September slipped rapidly away; a great many birds were left alive which ought to have been dead, because there was so much to do, so many rushes to London, so many absolutely necessary things to get before the start to Ireland.

The Boy wrote sheaves to the cousin, and the cousin sent short wires to say that he had secured 'digs'; beyond that he proffered no comment, but the Boy

equalized it by his pages of directions. The cousin was looked on as a species of father to the trip. The Boy spent his legacy lavishly, bought all things which he did and did not want. His face was a study as it looked from between the shoulders of his new pink coat. The house was crammed with packing-cases, with whips and sticks, and the smell of new leather oozed from every corner.

At length, on October 5th, you might have seen three men, pursued by porters who tottered under mountains of luggage, making their way down the platform at Euston. Fitzroy Travers, short, sturdy, clean-shaven; Kane-Norton, long-limbed, languid, an eyeglass fixed firmly in his eye (he saw perfectly), a long moustache drooping over his mouth; and the Boy, with his young face alight, his young voice harrying all the porters at once, and reducing the inspectors to despair by insisting on having a case full of saddles lifted off the weighing-machine, on the ground that it was personal luggage which he wanted to take in the carriage with him. The worried official suggested his paying for all the other seats, as no one else could possibly get in, but the Boy carried his point, as he was wont to do, and took the saddles.

They were finally settled; they disbursed much gold for extra luggage, and the white mail scuttled off into the crisp, still glory of an autumn night. Thundering past sleepy stations, pulling up now and again to fret and fume until it was once more away, roaring past the Welsh coast, where the lazy sea lapped the gray pebbles. Darting into the black depths of the Tubular Bridge, it finally stopped to cast out its load of sleepy passengers at Holy head, where the long mail-boat stood waiting; and then, in the gray dawning, the three came on deck as they steamed into Kingstown Harbour, and caught their first glimpse of the low green shores of the Emerald Isle.

It seemed little more than an hour since they had left England, yet they saw a vast difference. There was a wild bustle on the quay, an air of vague and useless helpfulness among many men;

there was much rolling of soft brogues and whining Dublin twang.

'Funny, that we should never have come over here,' said Travers as they passed across the quay and huddled, chilled and sleepy, into their carriage. 'The whole place is different, somehow. When do we start?' he asked the collector, as that somewhat grimy individual came for their tickets.

'Oh, ye'll be goin' presently. Presently, whin they have all on. Thank ye, sir. Ye'd better be takin' yer sates' — this to some loiterers outside. 'I'll see yer tickets now, plaze. Let ye go on up if ye're for Cork.'

The loquacious collector went on leisurely— mail-trains are made for man in Ireland—and presently, when 'she went on,' they steamed up past the sandy shore, the silvery sea crawling calmly over the flats, ran past and over the Irish capital, and 'into Kingsbridge Station.

By this time the Boy felt hungry, and being informed that breakfast would not be served until eight, he hailed a porter, asking for some tea, and was struck dumb by the heartiness of the reply. The porter came to the window, thrust a good-tempered face into the Boy's, and thus made answer:

'Tay, is it? Why not? Av course I'll have it for ye. The atin'-room is just above. Tay, I'll get it.'

'By Jove! they are good fellows, these Irish/ said the Boy enthusiastically. 'Imagine an English porter answering like that!'

He leant from the window, beaming on Ireland and waiting for his tea. But, as he watched, his enthusiasm grew fainter, for he saw his good-natured friend, caught as he drifted towards the refreshment-room, dump down a fellow-traveller's bag, and then rush to the assistance of a heated old lady who was striving to find something which she could not. The Boy leant out and hailed him with some asperity.

The porter turned and smiled. 'Oh, the tay—to be sure, to be sure! But she wasn't sthartin' on yit. In wan minute, whin I have this lady settled, I'll go for it; but in any case' —he began to drift

away again—' 'tis but a sthep to the re-freshment-room, and ye'll git it much hotter above.'

The Boy used many Saxon words, crisp and strong, before his tea arrived and was handed to him with a beaming smile and the assurance that 'there it was, afther all.' But his high opinion of the Irish was a little damped.

The mail rushed westwards, ever westwards, through low fields, between hedges of gorse, then through the great bog, wide-stretching, brown and desolate, with sheen of purple where the wind stirred its grasses. The pools lay sullen and desolate; stacks of turf were piled here and there, close by the deep cuttings it had been taken from. Then they ran into a grass land, intersected with sparse specks of brown plough, the fields fenced by low green banks. To the right rose a line of hills, their summits darkly purple, their sides flushing rosy from the sun's first kiss. The white mist still clung to the hollows. Cottages were dotted here and there; but save for these and the momentary bustle of the stations it was desolate—Desolate Ireland, with its own strange beauty.

'A country! What a country!' Travers threw the window wide. 'Look at it I Think of hounds across it 1' He seemed to feel Merrylass beneath him, stealing across those green pastures, now as they whirled past a fence—the lift of quarters as she flew the bank —then another. Oh, Travers, you knew not Ireland nor the depths of the ditches on either side of that tempting green fence: that knowledge was to come.

They chatted like magpies at breakfast, happy and excited. They were three men going to the Promised Land, scarcely knowing what wonders were before them.

'Change here for Cahirvally and the Oolagh line.'

They were bundled at length out on to a dirty platform at a long, straggling junction, and knew their journey was nearly over. The mail bustled fussily away from them, and they changed into a narrow carriage with dusty cushions. But what did dust matter? The grass country ran on every side. The Irish air,

soft as a caress, blew into their faces as they waited until someone should decide to start the train. High hills towered over them, the rich pastureland billowing towards their sides.

'I suppose your cousin '11 meet us, Boy,' said Travers when the train for Cahirvally took courage and proceeded. 'See us square and all that. If everything else is as cheap as those digs he's raised for us, we'll do this trip for nothing at all"

The Boy hoped so also, but dubiously: he knew his family.

Kane-Norton studied a time-table and announced that the next station was Cahirvally itself. They rushed like school-boys to the window. They were running through a tableland of pasture; in the west rose a range of hills which they learnt to know later; beyond these the towering Dullen Mountains. The train shrieked as it rushed round a bend and disclosed the town itself—a mass of gray buildings, with two long spires thrust boldly into the heavens, and nests of chimneys staining the air with their smoke.

'It's quite—a town.' Travers drummed on the window-pane, then delivered up his ticket as they stopped at a low platform. 'Somehow, I thought it was a village.'

The train drew up with a jerk in a dingy, dirty station, and they got out, to be engulfed in a flood of would-be helpers.

Travers said he would try to find the luggage, and, having engaged some six porters to assist, he struggled towards it. The other two were surrounded by an eager crowd of jarvey men. Cyar, sir? Want a cyar down, yer honours?

Me bye's ass '11 take the luggage. Here, sir L First cyar I am.'

Kane-Norton struggled wildly for the possession of his kit-bag. 'Upon my word, I don't understand them,' he said helplessly. 'Why didn't your cousin meet us, Boy? Oh, I say! for heaven's sake take one of their flys and have done with them. Yes, man, keep your fly for us'—this with emphasis to the brigand who had taken his bag.

'Glory be to God!'—it was the driver

who failed to understand now—' of coorse I'll fly, an' I'll be waitin' outside.'

Leaving their heavy luggage to Brown, Travers' man (who stood with an expression of resignation by the van, and occasionally received any portion of their property which a porter elected to throw at him), they arrived at the door to find three cars waiting for them. Finally, piling up light luggage to give colour to the mistake, they made a triumphal progress down the street, an ill-paved, ill-smelling place full of dirty children which rolled in the gutter with puppies and hens.

Kane-Norton and Travers clung warily to the sides of their several vehicles; the Boy balanced himself on his with some ease. They turned into a broader street; they pulled up with a flourish at a dingy, lofty house, the door of which was instantly swung open.

'Ye're welcome, gintlemen, welcome!' A smiling woman with a stern eye and a grimy dress came down the gray stone steps. ''Tis here Zz/tinant Clifford got ye yer rooms. Mrs. O'Neill I am. Hannah Anne, Hannah Anne! take this luggage above. Don't overpay thim robbers, now '—she indicated the three jarveys—' sixpince each is their full due.'

The Englishmen doubled this fare, and got into the house. A subtly-blended smell met them in the hall, of which the only recognisable parts seemed to be stale cabbage and old clothes. Their landlady led them up the dirty staircase, and ushered them into a big room looking out on to the street. A cheery fire blazed, and breakfast was ready laid near it.

'I have eggs fryin' for ye,' Mrs. O'Neill beamed, or, rather, her mouth beamed, and her eye remained stern. 'An' a taste of fryin' bacon an' Cahirvally sausages, for, faith, 'tis most convanient since the new thrains came in. Wan can always have things ready for about twenty minutes afther time. Not the ould late trains, indade, that 'ud sometimes sphite ye by bein' in before they were wanted. Will I carry up the breakfust for ye now?'

With some firmness Travers intimated that they would first have baths and plenty of hot water. Then they would partake of breakfast.

'A bath? Mrs. O'Neill's mouth beamed again. 'An,' sure, I have thim for ye. But I niver laid thim ready now, an' the eggs '11 be sphiled, an''

'Send up heaps of hot water,' said the Boy, quite unabashed by the stern eye which was having its effect on the other two; 'and be quick about it, if you can.'

Their landlady looked at him; then she vanished, and her voice was heard outside.

'Hannah Anne, Hannah Anne! empty the biler an' the big pot that's hatin' ready for the dinner potaties, an' hate the kittle, only kape a drhop in the little one convanient to wet the tay. Hurry on, Hannah Anne I Glory be to God! aren't the English terrible fond of washin'?"

CHAPTER II HOW THEY CAME TO THE GRASS LAND

Travers, Kane-Norton and the Boy took a heavy second breakfast, and, with the asperity born of slight indigestion, looked at their new abode as Hannah Anne removed the things from the table. It was probable that for many months they would start from this room to the joys of their grass country. The room was large, with three dirty windows looking out on to the street. Five chairs and a table made oases on a faded and unswept carpet. The paper peeled from the wall in many places—sometimes it was caught up with a patch of some other paper, sometimes not—and everything in the room wanted mending. But they supposed it to be typical, and regarded it with indulgence.

The street outside was wide and quiet. A little saddler's shop stood opposite; a few other tiny shops looked timidly out from the mass of tall gray houses. A few donkey-carts and heavy drays strayed up and down.

Mrs. O'Neill, breathing of the kitchen, interrupted them by pushing open the door.

'An' what will ye be afther havin' for the lunch?' she inquired.

They were just 'afther havin'' too much breakfast, and Travers, who was

the housekeeper, discussed the question languidly.

'Nothing much,' he said lazily. 'What have you got in? Cold beef or pressed beef, or cold

Mrs. O'Neill interrupted him hotly. 'Glory!' she said, 'and how would ye have anything cowld now, the day runnin' on to twelve? Be the time Hannah Anne had a twisht taken to the butchers an' we had it on below, 'twould be half an hour gone. Oh, faith, no. But if ye'll tell me what ye'd fancy'

Travers gave it up, and intimated that she might please herself. So, after a long soliloquy as to the respective merits of chickens and chops, delivered in an undertone at the door, she withdrew, and again her voice was heard uplifted outside as she bade Hannah Anne to 'scoot down to Carey's an' brin' back a fowl fit for the atin', an' to git a head of cabbage down at Delaney's stall, an' 'The remainder was lost in the depths of the kitchen stairs.

'Dear me!' said Kane-Norton weakly.

About ten minutes later Hannah Anne, with the chickens and cabbage under her arm, banged the door open, announced 'Liftinant Clifford! and fled again.

The author of the trip, a slight young fellow in undress uniform, came hurrying in. He hadn't a minute, he declared—only just ran down to see how they were all getting on. Deuced sporting of them, coming over like this! He hoped they'd find it value. 'I'd a rare hunt for these digs,' he went on, looking round. 'Norman '—they stared, then remembered that the Boy had a name—'Norman specified digs, or I should have thought that, at first, an' hotel'

'We quite thought this place was a mere village,' said Kane-Norton apologetically, ' and that the hotels would have been mere pot-houses. Or we should not have bothered you.'

'Oh, no bother at all. And you get your peck of dirt anywhere in Ireland. ' Clifford struck a chair with his cane, and a cloud of dust flew up. 'They clear out once a year or so. I went to five houses before I lighted on one where they possessed baths. It appears the old lady had some other English people here before who forced her to buy them. '

They forced him into a chair, and showered thanks and questions upon him. As to the meets? The distances? What to do on off days? Where to get horses?

Clifford resigned himself to fate, lit a cigarette, and puffed softly. 'The distances? Well, they are pretty bad; Cahirvally is on the edge of the hunting, so to speak, and I hear twenty miles is a mere nothing. Off days? Oh, shoot and fool round; the girls are rippers.' Here he became thoughtful. 'Where to get horses? My dear fellow, they grow on the trees; the jarvey who drove you here will sell you one '— (they thought of the three beasts which had drawn them down the stony street, and shook their heads)—' the shopmen keep them; every woman who hunts deals in them; every man's a horse-coper. They let their houses fall— one fellow told me he had to go out on windy days and lean his back against his to keep it up— but they ride superb cattle; and, by Jove! I hear they can go on them.'

The Boy then suggested introductions, having their names put down at the club, and so forth; but here Clifford appeared to wash his hands of them. He was going away for a day or two; when he came back he'd ask one of the seniors about it. 'They're very good and hospitable here—to soldiers,' said Clifford dubiously; 'but otherwise, I've been told, they will want to know who one is first, you know.'

Travers suggested with some heat that perhaps he had better send for his mother's marriage certificate, and the Boy, conscious of a long line of immoral ancestry, smiled softly.

'But you are sure to get on all right, hunting people, y' know.' Clifford, quite unconscious of offence, raised his kharki-clad form from the uneasy chair. 'You must dine directly I come back; I fancy they'll starve you here. Come up to barracks this afternoon; I'll be away, but Dickson will look after you. By-the-by, I believe Dickson is going out, but

I'll tell someone. So sorry I'm off myself! So glad I've been able to be of use to you! I hear the sport's quite good, so I'm sure you'll be glad you came. See you on Monday, Norman. Mind you come up this afternoon'

He was gone, and the three stared a little blankly at each other. They had depended a good deal on Clifford. They were strangers, knowing no one, and they felt at the moment as if even grass might not be worth it.

'Cool card, your cousin,' said Kane-Norton sourly.

'He didn't ask us over,' remarked the Boy, but the remark was palpably forced. 'Never mind, the place is rippin', and we're bound to settle down after a bit. If we'd gone down to the shires, I don't suppose we'd have known a soul.'

This philosophy cheered them up, and KaneNorton, finding the room stuffy, tried to open another window, but found it hermetically sealed. The Boy rang for Hannah Anne, and, getting no answer, kept on ringing. After some five minutes had elapsed, the damsel put in her head round the door and inquired if the gentlemen wanted her. Being informed, somewhat forcibly, that they did, and what was wrong, she giggled coyly, and ' thought the hate of the summer must have surely swhelled the paint, andsthuck the things, bad manners to it! for no one iver wanted more than wan windy open.'

Travers wanted to know why she hadn't come when they rang. Hannah Anne explained that 'she had twice thried the frontdoor, and thin took a squint at the bells to see if the rats was shakin' thim, and thin, hearin' a tramplin' up above, and the bell ringin' continuous '—the Boy had the clapper a foot from the wall, and was using his full strength—' faith, she'd come up an' seen it was them.' She was quite unabashed, and suggested no apology. Hannah Anne was a lady of somewhat full habit, with a plump bosom, a red face, and coarse black hair, adorned at the moment with a chevaux-de-frise of leaden hair-curlers. Having, with great interest, regarded a boy driving pigs

outside, she remarked that 'it was time to bring up the mate,' and withdrew.

The men were not hungry, but even if they had been, it is doubtful if they could have eaten much. Lunch was a meal more of quantity than quality. Two enormous chickens, unadorned by any dressing save a little greasy water, reposed, visibly ill at ease, on a thick dish. Magnificent potatoes, in their jackets, were heaped on a plate; and a third dish of the class called vegetable (which is generally suspicious as to cleanliness) was filled to the brim with cabbage, also dressed with water. Hannah Anne, telling them that she would be 'back prisintly with a taste of a swate,' dumped down some plates, gave the forks a last rub with her apron, blew the dust from some knives, and withdrew.

Travers took a knife, and set to work on the largest chicken. There was some difficulty in carving it, because its wings seemed to have got mixed up with its legs, and its legs were wound round its head or spread wildly. Fortunately, he was a strong man and patient, and after a while he helped Kane-Norton, and was giving some to the Boy, when Kane-Norton, who had been well brought up, observed that he thought it was an athletic bird, and had probably been running races no later than that morning, to strengthen its muscles for some forthcoming competition; and he helped himself to potatoes.

The Boy said more tersely, 'My God! what an old cock!' and also took potatoes; and off the excellent butter and an apple pie—which Hannah Anne slightly put them off by adjusting the pastry knob with her fingers as she came in— they lunched frugally. Hannah Anne remarked, as she removed the chickens, that 'the battherin' comin' across the say had the appetites fair swep' from thim, and those chickens were two fine Orpin'ton's, the yally feathers was on their necks an she bringin' thim in.'

When the fragments of the feast had been, cleared away, the day stretched wearily in front of them, and they summoned Mrs. O'Neill from the kitchen by the process of shrieking firmly down the stairs. (The clapper of the bell still lolled out unhappily, and Brown was lost amid the maze of their traps.)

Mrs. O'Neill entered with a trail of boiled cabbage clinging to her, and assumed a thoughtful air when questioned about the sights.

'Ould places to see?' she said. 'Well, now! Sure, the shops was fine, and for an afternoon outing people mostly took the afternoon thrains to Knockane or Cahirend; but 'twas on her mind that the thrains was gone out. There was fine sights ov ould castles to be seen at thim places, an' a river, and a gran' hotel where do they give ye the tay; but, indeed, she would advise thim, tired as they were, to see the streets an' the bridge'

The Boy went to the door and yelled for his hat; the others foHowed him.

'Turn to the left as ye passes the door, thin to the left agin, an' ye'll hit Mary Street,' Mrs. O'Neill called after them.

The Boy, hoping gravely that Mary Street might not hit them back, led the way. They turned down the next street as they had been directed. It was a broad street, but the smelt drove across it and met in the middle—a mingled reek of rotting vegetables, decaying meat, and many other things strange to them. Small shops, full of strange vegetables, long strangers to Mother Earth, overflowed into the road, would-be purchasers handling the wares freely. They recalled the wet cabbage and shuddered. Cows and sheep, their faces set in the late agony of death, hung in the butchers' shops, oozing blood on to the pavement. Meat was being cut up on dirty wooden slabs; the odour which came hurling from the chicken and fish shop sent their handkerchiefs to their noses. The 'fine Orpin'tons' had travelled from there.

It was evidently market-day, for the roadway was blocked with donkey-carts and horsecarts, and fat country-women elbowed each other as they clamoured for bargains at the shop door. Raw odours of whisky strayed from sundry public-houses, and drunken men lurched about good-humouredly, stopping to hold unsteady converse with other drunken men. They threaded their

way with some difficulty, for no one ever dreamed of making way for them. Jarveys sometimes came through the throng, shaving many old women, who always seemed to choose the centre of the road to count their change or speak with a friend. Across an intersecting street they could see the river, silver gray, and beyond it a stretch of trees, sombre gray under the soft gray sky.

'A wonderful country!' said Travers, running against the tenth person.

'And this, I presume, is Mary Street,'said the Boy, whirling round the corner, and butting into an old woman, who murmured, 'Glory be to God! I beg yer honour's pardin,' in tones of apology.

This was Mary Street—' the street. They learnt later that Cahirvally only possessed one. There were the quays, brimming with life, there were sundry branches leading off, but to the people there is only one place worth naming. It is 'the street'; they go up 'the street,' or down it, and they know it by no other name. Their first impression, as they left some few of the smells behind them, was one of general dinginess; the town seemed dressed in drab. Big gray houses stretched to the gray sky; the shops were dingy, no touch of brightness in their windows. The elder Cahirvally dames scurried up and down, holding their skirts high, long lists in their hands and anxious expressions on their faces, for a week's food had to be considered.

A big green-shuttered building with steep stone steps they decided must be a club; this in a short time became 'the' also. The men who strolled in and out wore breeches and gaiters, and as they passed the steps a breath of how 'she was the best youngster I've owned for years, I tell you,' reached their ears.

The younger women who peered in at the shop-windows were undoubtedly pretty; even Kane-Norton, who was a captious connoisseur, murmured that their complexions were 'surprisin'.'

It was at this point that the Boy disgraced himself.

'Great Scott! look at the Queens of Sheba,' he said breathlessly and stood stock-still. Four girls turned out of a

side-street, in which street, as they learnt later, the aspiring lover might give tea (poured out in thick cups) to his lady-love. All four girls were dressed alike, in pale-blue trailing dresses, topped by marvellous French hats, obviously made in Cahirvally. They were fair, with dazzling skins, and mops of frizzled hair down to their pretty noses. They talked loudly, and cast little coquettish glances (as if waiting for the admiration which they knew would waft down to them) up at the club steps.

The Boy said afterwards that they stood and smiled at him, but as he occupied the middle of the footpath, his eyes wide with admiration, they could scarcely pass without looking. They divided and swept past him on either side; a wave of blue and flowers and feathers, leaving a trail of cheap scent in its wake.

'It is to be hoped,' said Travers icily, as he pulled the Boy on, 'that they will think you are a lunatic, and that we're your keepers.'

'But have you ever seen such women—all in a lump?' said the Boy, whirling round like a teetotum to catch a last glimpse of the blue backs, and quite unabashed by the scolding. 'If you had them in town, they'd knock it silly.'

On being removed, still babbling, he quite declined to see anything peculiar in his conduct 'in a town where everyone used the middle of the road for a meeting-place.' When, during the winter, he was introduced to the Queens of Sheba, he was heard to remark pathetically that he couldn't walk through their accents, and he was content to admire them from afar.

'My word, that's pretty!' Travers paused to look at a glimpse of the Cahir, fussing openmouthed over a rim of rocks, muttering hoarsely as it ran. A bridge, old and gray, cut the view across, and beyond rose a range of hills, dim in the autumn haze. They looked at it through a gap in the grimy houses, across a quay covered with carts of turf.

Kane-Norton had lost one of his portmanteaus by the way, and he announced that he must buy a tie for church on the morrow, and also some collars, in case the missing luggage did not turn up. After examining several shops, they at last selected one with a large portion of its cheaper wares flowing out into the street. It was a large building with many curious windows. They elbowed their way into the shop through a strange crowd — bare-footed women wrapped in shawls, respectable old bodies clad in stuffy velvet cloaks, harassed ladies of the upper classes mingling with the throng.

There was no one to show them their way, and so they walked along, searching for ties, and pausing to listen to the buyers as they went. If a bare-footed Irishwoman were to buy a cloak at Worth's, she would offer 99 for a £100 garment, and refuse to give more. The shopmen are obliged to keep two prices for these customers, and always ask a penny more than they mean to take.

They paused to listen at a counter where everything small on earth seemed to be sold, and a concourse of women gathered to buy.

'Young man, I'll give ye fourpince for it.'

'It cost us fivepince, ma'am. God's thruth for ye!' came from the heated shopman.

Another woman pushed the purchaser aside. 'Young man, me a'nt, Mary Brady, the lasht day she was here bought this. An' it not bein the right shade, an' she only havin' taken the laste taste ov it, she's wantin' to have it changed 'She thrust some brick-red flannelette forward. 'What's that? See the walker, did ye say? Sure, can't ye do it yeself?'

'Look now, young man: I'll give ye fourpince ha'pinny. That's me lasht word, or I'm away to Maloney's. Will ye give it to me now?'

'Look here, avick: I want a haporth o' pins, sthrong wans. They're to put some picthers on the walls, an' wan's the Vargin, an' I couldn't have her fallin''

And through it all the harassed shopman— there was one to each ten women—engulfed as he was, preserved a semblance of goodhumour. This particular youth—a stripling of twenty—sold his yard of stuff at 'fourpince ha'pinny,' snubbed Mary Brady's niece, and gave a packet of pins guaranteed to hold up the 'Vargin,' all in a minute. And even when Mary Brady's niece (who had departed in a noisy fury showering much abuse upon him) came back and asked 'if she had left e'er a thing behind her,' he found breath to retort: 'Nothin', ma'am, save your blessin',' whereupon the lady retreated hastily.

'My soul! they're a wonderful nation,' said Kane-Norton enthusiastically. 'Why have we never known them before? So intelligent, so witty, so absolutely good-humoured!'

'I mistrust 'em, since I met that porter,' murmured the Boy.

'You can't mistrust their smartness. Why, an Englishman in that boy's place would have been a lunatic.' Kane-Norton drifted on looking for ties. 'No wonder we've never subdued the Irish. Hallo, here we are!' as he ran the ties to earth.

There was a certain peace here; no one seemed to want ties.

'Can I git ye anything, sir?' inquired the youth in attendance.

'Ties,' said Kane-Norton pleasantly. 'Silk. Black with some white, y' know. Rather good.'

The youth—he was a pallid boy with smeareddown hair and a greasy face—responded affably.

He dived into several boxes on the counter and returned, his hands full of gaudy scarves of purple and blue and green, all of which, as they were rejected, he declared, with evident disappointment, to be the very newest thing. Then he rummaged behind the counter and appeared again. When a goodly, many-hued pile lay on the counter, Kane-Norton screwed his glass into his eye and asked if ' they hadn't got any black and white ties.'

'This 'd match ye lovely.' The youth held a flaring scarlet in close proximity to KaneNorton's pallid cheeks, and admired the effect with rapture. 'Black? We have black, but not what 'd match ye. Anyhow, they're not worn now'

'Have you got them?' asked Kane-Norton sharply.

'Black an' white. Silk. Good.' The youth scratched his ear with his pencil. 'I'm afther believin' we had thim in wance; but here now' —he dived suddenly—' here's a rale nate tie ye haven't seen—yally, with'

'Why the devil, if you haven't got them, didn't you say before?' said Kane-Norton heatedly.

'With red shpots,' finished the youth, quite disregarding the interruption.

'Are they quite devoid of sense, these Irish?' muttered Kane-Norton, stiffening his neck as he heard splutters of laughter behind him. 'Now, look here'—he thought it was time to abandon trying to buy ties—' no, no! I don't want you to order them for me—I want some collars. What will you offer me?' He swung round angrily upon the Boy and Travers, but their faces were strangely grave. Yet there had been a chuckle somewhere, and it was certainly not the shopman; he was still mildly affable and anxious to sell. 'What will you offer me?' inquired Kane-Norton with polished sarcasm.

The youth grinned feebly; he turned to a brown-paper parcel, and fresh hope illumined his face. 'There's a box of brown ties, now, I've remimbered thim—the very latest from Dublin; ye could not object to thim,' he said, seemingly unable to banish ties from his mind.

'Collars!' roared Kane-Norton, losing his temper and his customary languor. 'Collars' —he spoke with laborious distinctness, as one might speak to the deaf or a foreigner. 'Sixteen inch. Stand-up. Not turn-down. May I ask if there is any difficulty in procuring them? Only, if there are not any in the shop, for heaven's sake say so at once.'

'Oh, an' faith,' said the youth, brightening up, 'but there's plinty in the shop.'

'Then, why won't you get them for me? Don't you see I'm waiting?' said Kane-Norton, striving, at the imminent risk of something giving way, to keep to the level of the greasy youth's intellect. 'Coll-ars—coll-ars. Why— don't— you—get—them?'

'Because, sure, they're sowld at the counther beyant there, where ye may see thim gray veshts hangin'.'

The eyeglass flew with a jerk from KaneNorton's eye. He rescued, but was too agitated to restore it. Then he struggled with many words which bubbled inaudibly in his mouth, and retreated with some dignity. But it was evident that a doubt as to whether the honours of war lay with him troubled his angry mind.

'Beyant, I tell ye, where thim gray veshts is,' piped a voice behind him. 'An' look here. If ye're so anxious for me to sarve ye, I'll come cross an' git those collars for ye. No wan 'll say a word for wance.'

I doubt if to this day that youth knows how near he was to a violent end, as they left him plunging lightly across the counter while KaneNorton, his head erect, his eyeglass dangling, cleft a path through many old women: he did not wait to hear any more Irish wit.

At the door, where oilcloth and shawls and a few penny hats tumbled happily together, he paused. The Boy and Travers had abandoned themselves to laughter, and rocked upon the pavement.

Il think,' said Kane-Norton icily, 'we'll go to the barracks. Here, you carman! For heaven's sake drive us up to where we'll find some English people, and—some ordinary intelligence.'

'The barracks—infantry,' directed the Boy, clinging to the car as they cleared a crossing by some two feet, and bumped down again in a splatter of mud. (Cahirvally streets are always dirty.) 'Perhaps we'll find someone there who won't offer us prussic acid when we want whisky, and say it's quite the latest poison from Dublin, which will "match us lovely." Oh those collars! Coll-ars—white—stand-up, not sit-down—and that youth, who is still, doubtless, waiting patiently by the " veshts "! Here, hold on, you driver! don't upset us!'

'Arrah!' said the jarvey contemptuously, and drove them forwards at a full gallop.

CHAPTER III OF THE HORSES WHICH DID NOT GROW ON THE TREES

When Travers, Kane-Norton, and the Boy had spent nearly a week at Cahirvally, they began to settle down. They learnt to disregard Mrs. O'Neill's stern eye and to mistrust her cooking. They learnt that, as man must have his peck of dirt, he might as well get it all at once in Irish lodgings. They took long walks into the country, and stood rapturously on the low fences near the town, and looked happily across the slopes of sound pasture stretching away to the hills. The Boy's cousin had taken more trouble than he had appeared to, and a warm welcome had awaited them in barracks. Kane-Norton strove to forget the collars there, and might have succeeded if the Boy had not told the tale. They were admitted presently behind the green portals of the club, and met the country magnates, whom they were to ride against in the winter, and who received them cordially even without their family trees. They tried, vainly, to sort the family of Doyle, who seemed to overflow the place, from Connor Doyle, fat and sixty, down to young Connor Doyle, who was not yet sixteen. They met Dick Doyle and Donovan Moore, the rival thrusters of the county — the former short, red-headed, full of geniality; the latter long, lean, saturnine, with a snarling voice and gray eyes which looked with suspicion upon all outsiders.

Doyle and Moore were consistent enemies and rivals, save when they met on the common ground of impressing a stranger with the idea that there was but one hunting-ground, and Cahirvally was its name. There were tales, too, in the sparsely furnished club smokingroom, which set the Englishmen gasping, and made Travers wonder once or twice whether he was quite wise to risk Merrylass across such a country. For forty minutes fast was nothing —a mere morning breather. There were tales of brown bog, where a horse—but it must be an Irish horse, and for choice one of Moore's or Doyle's—went squelching up to its hocks in the moist turfy soil, and yet could shoot like a deer across fifteen feet of sullen water. 'Bottomless, sir, bottomless, the take-off a morass, and we landed with a foot to spare.'

Tales of stone walls—the Englishmen blinked, knowing not stone walls—five feet and upwards, mason-built. Tales of banks, razor-topped, flanked by watery graves, where a horse must combine goat and cat to change his feet on the slippery top.

'There are moments when I think I'll walk,' said Travers solemnly one night, as they came home from barracks through the empty, illlighted streets. Champagne had brightened the Cahirvally imaginations, and touched the stories with an extra tint of rose.

'We're no use; we should lie about England, said the Boy discontentedly. 'Begad, if we don't, they'll begin to think they're the only liars in the world. '

As yet they had not found any of the bargains in horse-flesh which were to make their fortunes. If horses grew on the trees, they were very hard to pick off. A friendly Major had whispered to them to say nothing of their wants in the club. Nearly every man there could sell them a horse, and to reject what was offered might mean enmity for the winter. The thought of being coldly regarded by the whole Doyle clan for five months made them shudder.

Travers made friends with jarveys by grossly overpaying them, and these jarveys always knew a man who just had had a horse, or another who would soon be 'afther havin' wan.' They found nothing actually ready. When it was discovered that they were 'on the buy,' several horses turned up, and Hannah Anne announced more than once that there was 'a felly wid a baste for sale below.'

The first one was regarded with some interest. He was a big black, quite in the rough, and bestridden by a ragged countryman. They gathered round him in the street, their souls athirst for bargains.

'Has he been jumped?

'Jumped, is it? Look here, yer honour: ye couldn't knock him. I rode him all lasht winther. Put him up on the narryest bank ye can find, an' I'll engage he'll dance a jig for ye above on it.'

The Boy, always captious, thought it might perhaps be 'better if he went on into the next field/ and was squashed by Kane-Norton, who said sharply 'that was only the man's way of puttin' it.'

'An' walls, begob!' pursued the owner. 'Ye might ride him at houses, an' he'll lay the legs on thim as nate, just a touch, to be sure there's nothin' beyant. '

It sounded well. They told the man to trot the horse down the road, and as he did so an ominous noise reached their ears.

'Surely'—Travers didn't like to put it more severely to the beaming owner— 'he makes a noise.'

'A n'ise, is it? He's the soundest horse in his wind iver ye saw. That's a feed of turnips I was fool enough to guv him afore we stharted, so that he might be lookin' gay like, an' 'tis full he is.'

He trotted again. The horse was an undoubted roarer. On this point being brought home, the man gave in reluctantly —' that maybe he did make a thrifle of a n'ise'—he now forgot the turnips—' but, sure, that niver sthopped him an' if their honours would only see him jump 'But he was despatched, grumbling, and subsequent callers met the same fate; none of the 'bastes' came up to the standard of their requirements.

They went to a local horse-dealer, a fat, affable person, and came away with a higher opinion of Irish horses and their value. Mr. Cassidy's stud was far above their price. They were directed to a small dealer who was very deaf, and in consequence whispered confidentially into his customers' ears, the logic of this action being difficult to find. He had nothing, either, though he promised to find them something.

Travers was beginning to despair and think of falling back on the Doyle family, when their favourite jarvey—the brigand who had snatched Kane-Norton's bag—came to the rescue with a suggestion.

'The dogs,' he informed them,'would be out huntin' at Ballyhale on Thursday, an' a power of harrses 'd be out. There were Jimmy Casey and his brother, who always owned something good." He would drive them out, and they could look at their leisure.

This rang sound, and at six-thirty on Thursday they started, leaving Hannah Anne a crushed damsel upon the doorstep, 'becaise they wouldn't wait on the hot wather' until their return.

'Sure, I was up the blessid night,' she complained, 'hatin' the kittle. The want of slape 'll be in me eyes for days.' She rubbed these organs wearily. 'An' the missus screechin' at five, an' scoldin' becaise I wint an' lay down on me bed for wan minute' (these statements did not seem to hang together). 'An' glory be, wouldn't the bath have done ye as well whin ye came in?' finished Hannah Anne, wiping a little spare grime from her face with the corner of her ever-useful apron.

It was a long drive through the chill October morning. Mist wraiths clung in the hollows; the hedges were full of berries and fading leaves. The sky flushed to rose in the east, where a pale sun thought of rising. They drove along narrow roads past stretches of peaceful country, occasionally passing cottages where, as the day woke, they saw the sleepy country people driving in their cows to milk, and rosy, towy-headed children stared at them as they drove by. They turned at last from the flat tableland, and drove through a succession of humpy hills rising steeply from boggy land, and sloping upwards till they gathered into a small mountain. But it was a glorious country. Clifford had not exaggerated. Grass, all grass— sound old pasture fenced by green banks and loose stone walls. It was a line for a hunting man to dream of.

The big gray mare in the shafts covered the ground with her swinging trot. She was blind of one eye, and otherwise unsound, but she champed at her bit and made light of her load and the ten miles she had to cover. The driver turned in at an iron gate.

'Here's Ballyhale,' he announced; 'an' there's the dogs an' the masther.'

The hounds, old Sir Ralph Clifford with them, came trotting across; he nodded to them as he passed.

'Thought you said you'd plenty of foxes for us this year?' The M. F. H. turned to a tall, heavily bearded man who was on foot by the gate.

Oh, heaps, Sir Ralph—heaps indeed,' he answered uneasily.

Sir Ralph gave him a peppery glance.

'They don't seem to have much smell,' he muttered, lashing the laurels savagely.

The master was a lean, gray-haired little man, somewhat famous for his command of language. He rode magnificent horses, and nothing could stop him. His daughter, also lean and small, rode close to him, mounted on a roan cob, which, the jarvey whispered confidentially, 'faith, ye might turn within there, an' be sure ov gittin' over.' 'There1 was a wall, about ten feet high, leading out of the wood, with a wide ditch on the taking-offside; but the man — his name was Maddigan — evidently meant what he said. Maddigan proceeded in whispers to point out celebrities to them:

'Him on foot, now, that's Misther Moloney, the owner ov the place, an', faith, they does say that he puts a tashte ov powther in the foxes— that's why Sir Ralph was short-like. Her above on that gran' bay, that's Miss Maguire, the orphint, with a fine house an' a power of money, an' the divil a thing she cares for beyant follyin' the dogs.' He indicated a big, squarely-built girl with a freckled face and shrewd eyes, riding a splendid-looking bay. 'An' there's Mrs. Martin, the besht in the hunt, an' Misther Hanlon wid her—she rides afther him; an' Dick Doyle—but, sure, ye know him; an' ould Connor—fat as he is, ov they were runnin', ye'd be glad to be near him—an' young Masther Connor. Glory! 'tis a fine mate.' Now, this was information, but it was not horse-coping; but suddenly Maddigan bent and whispered again: There's Mike Casey himself, an' on a young horse, too, an' his brother out on the ould racehorse. Look, Captain, look! that wan himself might match ye.'

Mike Casey was a slight, wiry little man, clean-shaven, with deep-red hair and the shiftiest eye, perhaps, ever seen in a human face; for the rest, his expression was one of childlike candour, as one who would say: 'Look at me. Is it possible that I could cheat you?' His brother was darker, with a long beard, and generally drunk, but so perfect a horseman that, unless the whisky absolutely rendered his legs incapable of holding on, he was about the hardest man to beat with the hounds.

The 'ould racehorse' did not interest them, but they looked long at the young horse which Mike Casey bestrode. It was a raking bay colt with great quarters and hocks, and a somewhat common head. The birds of the air may have told Casey that there were men out looking for horses; he came past them at an easy canter, sitting carelessly, the reins on the bay's neck, Kane-Norton's eye lit; he loved size.

'Nice colt that,' he whispered; 'quite in the rough, of course. These idiots over here never dream of trimming a horse up. Wouldn't do either of you, of course—too big '—this rather hastily. 'I wonder what he wants for him.'

A hound opened close to them, then another, until the wood rang with the chorus.

'By Jove! they've actually found,' cried Sir Ralph excitedly. A cub burst across the avenue, and, declining to be headed, made for a distant wood; with a burst of bloodthirsty music, hounds dashed out close on his brush.

The country people all seemed to go suddenly mad. Maddigan, the driver, sprang on to the box-seat of the car with an ear-splitting yell to 'git up, git up!' (they had all been down watching the crowd). The three men flung themselves at the seats, but long before they could get securely seated they were off, at a raking gallop, in the thick of the crowd of horses. The Boy lay on his stomach across the well, unable to regain his balance because Travers was sitting on his legs. Kane-Norton, much perturbed, with the eyeglass floating in the breeze, trailed behind, hopping, one foot on the step, the other on the ground, his hands clinging wildly to the rail. Maddigan urged the mare to her full speed, with running comments on the hunt as he shook the whip.

'They're over the sunk fince. Oh, my, my! We musht make the gate; isn't that terrible! Well over! Begob! Well done, miss! Miss Maguire's the girl! Well done, ould Connor! Good agin! Holy Vargin, there's wan down! Look: there's McClintock makin' the gate! Lave it open, man—lave it open!'

Kane-Norton swung on to the car just in time to see Casey on the bay clear the sunk fence in style. Travers, finding his cushion restive and very noisy, moved, and the Boy, purple of visage, and declaring he could never digest food again, got to his knees on the well, clinging to Maddigan's shoulder as their wild progress continued.

'He'll be across the road,1 the driver shouted. 'On wid ye, ye decaiver!' The 'decaiver' lengthened her stride in obedience.

'Mind the gate, man! Look outl There!'

A wild yell from Kane-Norton. A pair of gaitered legs sawing the air as he pitched himself backwards, nearly upsetting the Boy, who in his turn clasped Maddigan round the neck, and almost pulled him down. They had swung through the gate at full speed, with a clang of catching metal.

'Arrah! Did the sthep touch? inquired Maddigan mildly. 'Ye naden't be so timorous. Sure, she's that egcited 'tis hard to guide her.' The reins at the moment were flapping loosely in the breeze. 'They're through the far gate,' he cried. 'We'll head them outside.' They tore through the wide gate just as the hounds poured out over the low wall.

Jumping off the car, the three scrambled across the bank at the far side of the road, and rushed up the field. Kane-Norton's eyes were all for the bay colt. He saw it jump off the road cleverly. Casey pulled it to a trot now, going up the field beyond. The next bank was a nasty one, high, blind, and uphill; the bay jogged up, propped himself, and went on and off lightly. Kane-Norton felt the pride of possession in his breast. He would have that bay.

The Boy, young and lean, breasted the hill gallantly, but poor Pug's race was nearly run; he turned, was headed and headed again, and met his death with a snarl of impotent agony, to blood the puppies hunting him.

'Good Lord! one would think they wanted to run him into the very jaws of the hounds,' said the Boy, open-eyed; he had never been out cubbing before. 'Queer lot, these Irish!'

'What else do you think they wanted to do? remarked a voice in his ear. It was Miss Maguire, the 'orphint,' sitting squarely on her big bay horse, and looking at him with amused eyes.

'Why, make him run, of course,' said the Boy, unabashed at having spoken his thoughts aloud.

'Are you coming to hunt here?' she asked.

'Rather!' said the Boy; 'I believe it's a fine place—in winter.'

'Then we'll show you some sport,' said Miss Maguire, moving on. 'When we do make them run.' She smiled a little superciliously.

In the meantime Maddigan, having left the mare to a boy on the road and joined the chase, had spoken what he called 'a few words' to Mike Casey, which resulted in an immediate invitation to go and see what horses the man had for sale. So the gray, none the worse for her gallop, trotted on again. The Caseys took a short-cut across the fields, and, after another long drive through narrow, desolate roads, they turned down a ' boreen,' and pulled up at the door of a solid-looking farmhouse, painted white, and with some pretensions to gentility. A heavy-waisted damsel greeted them, and, observing that her husband was in the stable and would come in directly, asked them in the meantime to have a cup of ' tay.' The cup of 'tay' resolved itself into a breakfast of boiled eggs and fried eggs, and much fat bacon, fried and smoking hot, all eaten to an accompaniment of hot buttered soda loaf. They had partaken lightly in the morning, and did justice to the meal. The Boy, after his fourth egg, mourned for his injured digestion and subsequent loss of appetite.

No one came near them until they had finished, and then, as neatly as if he had been peeping through a spyhole, Mike Casey made his appearance. He could show them every class, he told them confidentially—all his remarks were made in this tone—but, as they were new to the country, he strongly advised them to buy made horses. He led the way through a dirty yard to a range of neat boxes; a couple of helpers were hissing vigorously over the two horses which had come in from hunting.

There were several hunters to look at, and Travers' eye was instantly caught by a well-bred black mare, fired for curbs, but with the best shoulders he had ever seen, and, Casey declared, a perfect jumper. She was brought out and trotted down the yard, moving well, with the easy action which stamps breeding.

'Get up and try her, sir,' urged Casey, pointing to the fences which lay all round. 'You won't find her make a mistake.'

A snaffle bridle was put in the mare's mouth, and, nothing loath, Travers got on. He rode well, and he liked the mare's easy stealing movements as she cantered down the field. He saw a small green fence in front, and put her at it, sitting loosely for the fly. The mare was a sticky fencer when not with hounds; she cantered up, but propped well in the middle of the bank, a pause which Travers had never bargained for. He landed in an attitude more suggestive of affection than good horsemanship, with his arms tightly clasped round the mare's neck.

'Do they always sit down in the middle over a little thing like that?' he inquired irritably, as he dived for a lost stirrup.

Casey swallowed a grin, and remarked that it was usual; otherwise they would certainly fall.

Travers balanced himself for the next bank, and then flew, with speed enough to please him, a couple of stone walls. Fortunately, the mare did not buck over them. He came back without his cap, but his eyes shone. He vowed that it was a ripping country; that all Cahirvally men were liars when they said it was hard to cross; and Casey knew his mare was sold.

The price proved to be by no means

unreasonable. Not quite, perhaps, what they had been led to expect, but cheap in their eyes. Casey thought of future purchases, and so, after some small haggling, the mare, subject to her being sound, was bought and sold.

'I shall make on her,' said Travers, watching her shining black quarters as she was led away.

'You won't,' said Kane-Norton crossly. 'You're mad for made horses. I can't afford this trip unless I can make my expenses.'

He returned to the stables. The bay had just been done up, and was standing feeding. A horse never looks so well as in his own stable, his quarters towards you. The bay's coat shone; he was undoubtedly a good doer, for he thrust his nose down into his manger hungrily. But, to Kane-Norton's surprise, Casey did not seem anxious to sell.

'I've got a nice chestnut,' he said, measuring Kane-Norton's weight with his eye. 'This horse is not trained. He's not made.'

'I've seen him jump,' said Kane-Norton with an astute smile. He began to see. The bay was so good that the Caseys wished to keep him until he was older.

'But don't you want to sell?' he inquired.

'Oh, faith, I want to sell everything,' said Casey, grinning; 'but the chestnut. He would carry you.'

Kane-Norton would have none of the chestnut, then. He knew a horse when he saw one.

The Boy yawned and wandered away. He also wanted to buy a horse, but no one seemed to have any time to help him. He knew little about horses, but all horses were beasts with four legs, and he was bored. He remarked this aloud in his usual way, and was overheard by the younger Casey, who came across the road, redolent of whisky; he also had been taking a second breakfast.

'I'm only learning,' said the Boy disconsolately. 'I want something that will take me along. I must leave the money-making to later on.'

James Casey grinned, and took the Boy by the arm. He led him away to a stable in a corner away from the others.

'Here's what '11 match ye,' he said as he opened the door. 'Buy this felly'—whisky curtailed his speech. 'Here, I'll show him to ye, but don't expect to see too much.'

The rugs were pulled off, and the Boy saw the 'fellow,' a small gray with high, ragged hips and good shoulders, his lean, well-bred head well set on. It was hard to say what his legs might have looked like originally; he had been fired for most things, and blistered for the rest. He was stiff as a crutch as he moved round the stable.

'Lave his legs alone—buy him,' said James Casey, breathing whisky and good-humour all round him. 'He can't fall; he can't tire. Ye can sthick a curb on him, or no bridle at all. He'll care ye, for he's used to carry a dhrunkard, an' he had to care him. I only got him be chance whin a man died, and I was loath to see him go to a common car. Ye can have him for thirty pound; that's five on me bargain' (for all his affability, it was probably nearer fifteen. The Caseys, drunk or sober, never forgot themselves). 'Thirty pound, an' they'll be whistlin' for yer heels across the counthry. 'Tis thruth I'm tellin' ye. I niver yit thried to come over a man who didn't thry to come over me. If people thinks they knows too much, sure 'tis only Christian charity to undecaive thim. Take him now, sir, an' don't be lookin" at him—he niver was a beauty—an' give him back to me av ye knocks him.'

'By Jove! I'll close,' cried the Boy excitedly. 'If you give me a fiver back for luck.'

James, dryly remarking that he had 'the makin' ov a horse-daler in him,' split the difference, and the bargain was made. Vets, needless to say, were superfluous, for, except his wind, there was nothing sound about the horse.

Flushed and excited, and just a little nervous, the Boy went back to the others.

Kane-Norton had made his bargain, and stood rapturously contemplating the bay colt. In imagination he was already spending the money which he would make on him. The Caseys had not, to his surprise, asked a big price. They had offered him several other horses, but he would have none of them. They were likewise lukewarm about any trial. Kane-Norton had 'seen the horse out; he knew how he could jump. They could guarantee his soundness, but the horse was still green'

Kane-Norton smiled in a superior manner, and bought the colt—Four years, by Glenmartin, sixteen hands, well up to fourteen stone, undeniably handsome.

Kane-Norton thought he was beginning well.

Travers by this time had almost decided on another, a chestnut six-year-old; but it made a noise, so he was to be given a day's hunting before he decided. Then, as they were being taken to the house for further refreshments, they recalled the Boy, who had also wanted a horse and been forgotten.

'But I've got a horse, thank you,' said the Boy loftily.

'He's bought ould Tim,' said James Casey unsteadily.

They came to stare at the screw and hurt much abuse on the Boy, but Mike Casey assured them that, whatever the horse might be like to look at, he was quite undefeatable across a country, and that, 'if the young gentleman wanted to see sport, he couldn't have done better.

'He must know a horse when he sees one,' said the elder Casey, and the Boy drew himself up proudly.

He refused to be cast down or abashed, and determined to abide by his bargain. And, moreover, he excited James's further admiration by swallowing a glass of whisky without a wink.

All the way home the Boy bore the laughter and the contempt they treated him to. KaneNorton babbled happily of how he had made the Caseys sell, only pausing to abuse the Boy.

'They thought I didn't know a valuable horse when I see one,' said Kane-Norton. Then, 'Boy, why didn't you wait for me? Why on earth did you let yourself be cheated by that drunken brother?'

The Boy took it all patiently. Was not the day to come when they would be 'whistlin' for his heels across the counthry'? He hugged this thought and was silent.

CHAPTER IV OF SOME SERVANTS AND A FOX CHASE

When a man buys horses he must find someone to mind them. The three men who had come to hunt at Cahirvally remembered this. The man who had come with them partook more of the nature of a body-servant than a groom; he wrestled with Hannah Anne in the kitchen because she would put their boots to dry in the oven and hang their coats across the dirty platerack to air. Also, when the bell sounded, she could be heard arguing on the stairs when he attempted to answer it.

'An' what in the name ov God d'ye think I'm paid for!' the stout damsel would shrill contemptuously. 'Let ye go back now, Misther Brown, and lave me to me own worrk, av ye plaze.' Then, remarking further that 'there was a sight ov boots to be schraped below, an" the dusty clothes crying out to be brushed,' she would make her leisurely way upstairs, and arrive by the time they had lost patience and almost forgotten what they wanted. Ireland was teaching them many things.

But to return to grooms. Merrylass, pride of her master's heart, was due to arrive on Thursday from England; the Caseys' horses were to be examined on Tuesday and come in next day. So it was time to do something. Merrylass's own boy was coming over with her; they wanted two other men. KaneNorton, who rather prided himself on his management of servants, and considered that Travers, the easy-going, would never do to wrestle with the Irish character, undertook to interview the various candidates. Maddigan had been informed of their wants, and an advertisement inserted in the *Cahirvally Moderator*. The front-door bell rang 'continuous '; even the best of leaden hairpins failed to keep Hannah Anne's locks in curl; her state of mind, as she swarmed to the door, almost washed the grime from her face. The menage at No. 8, Connel Street, did not improve; they grew weary of bacon and eggs for breakfast, and nothing else could be provided. The butcher was a hard-hearted man, sending them slabs of hard steak, and mutton cut from the largest sheep in the world. It was, apparently, always 'killin' day,' and the 'mate' in consequence a ' thrifle fresh.'

They dined nightly at the club, where the cooking was passable, and they played billiards on a table which Noah had learnt the game on.

'There's a young man at the dour who wishes to see ye. His name an' bizness? Wisha now, didn't I say he wanted to see ye?' Hannah Anne would stump down grumbling. After an hour or two, she put in of her own accord, ' a young man afther the place,' and thus saved her stout legs a journey.

The first 'young man,' a collarless youth of about twenty-one, with an ingenuous face, stood at the doorway bashfully. Kane-Norton, judicial, very dignified (because the Boy suggested the grooms might be like the shopboy, a little hard to manage), his eyeglass wedged firmly in his eye, awaited the applicant. Travers sat in the doubtful chair, smoking. The Boy warmed himself at the fire, and the interview proceeded.

'You've come about the place?'

'I have, yer honour.'

'I suppose you have recommendations'— they had discovered this was the Irish fashion —' let me see them.'

'An' sure I have'—triumphantly. 'Father Magee, who knew me father well—God rest his sowl!—guv me a bit ov a note, and I was above at Murphy's for six months carin" the pony, an''

'But my advertisement said hunters. Hunters!' (' He'll soon get to hunters, sixteen hands, not ponies,' whispered the Boy.) 'Have you ever looked after hunters?'

'Well, thin, faith, no, sir, I niver had raison to. But, sure, I cared Murphy's pony splindid, as ye'll see there; an' pigs he had, and I fed thim'

'Good God!' The eyeglass showed signs of falling. 'If that's all—you can go.'

'Where, sir?'

Michael Kelly—his name was writ on his papers—grew bright with hope.

'To the devil, if you choose!' remarked Kane-Norton savagely.

'Thank ye, sir.' The youth looked round as if seeking that gentleman.

'You wouldn't thry me yerself, sir?' in insinuating tones. 'Sure, ov I couldn't exactly care the hunthers, I could clane thim fine, sir; I'm not afraid of work.'

He was at last despatched, but he insisted on leaving his address behind him, in case they changed their minds and gave a further reference to Murphy's pony.

The next youth had not minded hunters, either, but he impressed it on them that he had lived adjacent to them—next door, in fact—and 'seen thim goin' out to exercise reg'lar'; and he also had a line from his parish priest.

It was really wonderful, looking at the ragged clothes and mischievous faces of the grooms who poured in, how many strictly honest and sober lads Ireland managed to turn out.

The eyeglass fell many times during that day. Kane-Norton's slow English voice showed signs of giving out, his far from slow English temper signs of wearing thin, and the flow of applicants continued. Eventually he gave it up, and just as the Boy, fresh from a walk, took up the running, beginning with a cheery, 'Here! what the dickens do you know about hunters?' a suitable man, of reasonable years, turned up, was promptly engaged as groom by the weary men, and asked to engage a boy for himself. He inclined, strange to say, to Michael Kelly, the youth who had 'cared Murphy's pony,'because, as Cassidy said, 'he knew nothin', an' would have nothin' to unlearn'; also, 'his people were dacent, and had in days gone by lived next door to his (Cassidy's) people'— a perfect hall-mark, apparently, of' dacency.'

Michael was speedily found; in fact, it seemed as if he had lingered outside, in hopes still that the devil he had been sent to was some other occult name for Kane-Norton's stables.

So everything was redy when Travers received a wire from James to say that Merrylass, the precious, and the one reserved by Kane-Norton, had actually started and were on their way across.

The horses were due to arrive by the one o'clock train, and Travers went alone to the station. Kane-Norton and the Boy were out bringing in the new stud, which had passed their examinations with flying colours. Travers saw the train come, but, to his astonishment, there were on horses on it, and no one else seemed astonished. The porters thought ''twas likely the horse-box would come in on the six; in fact, 'twas probable they would.' The station-master, on being hotly interrogated, thought the same, and recommended patience until then.

''Twas no manner of use,' he said, 'to be wirin' round the counthry. God knew where thim horses might be now.'

Travers, in consequence, passed an uneasy day, imagining all kinds of disasters to his marc, and long before six he was off to the station again, accompanied this time by the other two, who had arrived back with the new horses.

They were much too early, and met on the platform Miss Maguire, escorted by Doyle and Moore.

Both these hard-riding men were bachelors, and it looked, from the sour glances they cast at each other, as if they both aspired to the heiress.

Sheila Maguire was a big, squarely-built girl, attractive, without having any real claim to good looks, her abundant light-brown hair and fine skin being her best gifts. Her well-made coat and skirt fell loosely over her spare figure, clearing by quite two inches her strong, unlovely boots. Yet the dress was plainly built by a master-hand, and suited its wearer well. Doyle wheeled her bicycle; Moore carried a couple of small parcels.

Miss Maguire looked at the three Englishmen as they came up, and whispered something to Doyle, who introduced her. She nodded to the others, but turned at once to the Boy.

'So you're the one who objects to seeing foxes killed?' she said.

Her voice was soft, with a touch of

the Southern brogue in it.

'No, no; not bein' killed—hounded to death/ answered the Boy, unabashed, as usual, though he stood a stranger arraigned at the bar of sport. 'Hunt 'em down, if you're able. I never saw cubbin' before, and it seemed unfair —to me.'

'H'm! I don't know that I ever looked at it in that light,' she said, considering him with her good-humoured gray eyes.

'It's to be hoped you won't again,' snarled Donovan Moore, bestowing a hearty glance of contempt on the Boy.

The Boy returned it with a disarming smile. He thought of Ould Tim, who had hobbled in to-day lame all round. To his rapid imagination it was possible that these two fliers of Cahirvally might ' whistle for his heels' with the rest.

Moore received the smile on a lance of cold distrust, and elbowed the Boy aside.

Travers had gone a little away, and aired his grievances at some length, when a flustered porter came tearing down to announce that 'the six was in, an' a thruck behind her; an" surely 'twas the horses the gintleman expected.'

Miss Maguire looked at her watch, remarked that they had time to go round to see the English mare, then, with a careless word to the guard to keep the train if she was late, she followed Travers down the platform.

The 'six' stood steaming by the platform, disgorging its load. Travers bustled through the crowd in the tail of the important porter.

'But—it's a truck!' he cried, as he saw it. 'A truck!' He darted forward. 'Is everyone mad?'

The engine grunted, and shunted the truck on to a dark platform a little further out.

Merrylass, his valuable mare, coming over from England in a truck! Travers fumed wildly, and the others followed him.

The porter opened the door and they peered in. There was a hazy vision in the dimness of a horse without any rugs on.

'Stolen!' cried Travers. 'The clothing is stolen!' and he babbled excitedly of damages.

Kane-Norton lost his languor and became excited now. Were his things also stolen? Also the murky shadow seemed only to hold one horse.

'Wan,' said the porter's voice from the warm dimness of the truck. 'Well, 'tis all I can see; unless, maybe 'There came the splutter of a match, and a little spurt of yellow flame bit through the darkness. 'Faith, an' I can't see another wan inywhere,' said the porter stolidly, waving his little arc of light.

As the chuckle which followed this remark died away, another match spluttered, and a yell from Travers drowned everything. This sheetless horse was *not* Merrylass, but an old brood mare—a portly lady with a long tail and pendulous under-lip, who regarded the wildly excited maa with a mildly indulgent eye.

A moment later the pavement of the Cahirvally station echoed to the frantic stamping of two pairs of brown boots, the dirty roof rang to the notes of two furious Saxon voices:

'Where? When? How? Where were Merrylass and Blackbird? What the'

Miss Maguire, listening with interest, remarked that she thought Travers would make an excellent master of hounds. Then she strolled off to her train, which had waited for ten minutes, hooting wearily on the far platform.

The Boy came with her, calmly ousting her attendants. They would not have taken it meekly if they had not been engaged in attending to the spirited argument which echoed and rolled up and down by the truck, gathering force as official after official strolled down to see if there was anyone extra drunk.

'I can do no good here,' he remarked. 'See you to your train. My word! they are a queer lot, these Irish!'

'So I've heard before,' said Miss Maguire dryly.

But she shook hands with him at parting, after he had put all her parcels in, and politely swept away a cloaked old country-woman who sought for a first-class place in the overcrowded train, with the ready remark that this wasn't her train at all—she must go lower down if she wanted to get home; at which the old lady fled with many blessings on his head.

In the meantime Travers and Kane-Norton had stormed various offices, gathering up a train of more or less innocent officials as they went, to be met in every quarter by stolid imperturbability.

'Twas likely the horses had gone on somewheres. Maybe the box was changed in Dublin, or at Oolagh, bechance. An' if so, the hunthers 'd be surely at Darriveen, or if they weren't there, faith, 'twas unbeknownst. Wire? Oh, to be sure! But 'twas that late, an' on thim side-lines 'twasn't likely there'd be a train to pull thim down till the mornin'. Would they be looked after? Will, thin, ov they chanced on a place where there was a taste of sthuff to feed thim with, they'd surely get it; but in thim small places 'twas hard to say.

At last, when Travers was hoarse, and to remain longer would have been to lay the bearded station-master and the fat booking-clerk dead on the platform, they went home. They were too agitated to go out, and Mrs.

O'Neill had her peace of mind disturbed by a suddenly ordered dinner. Hannah Anne promptly took her usual 'twisht' to the butcher's, where, as usual, it was killing-day— 'the divil fly away with them '—and procured chops, which had clearly been sheep that morning. These chops lay heavily on their minds. And Hannah Anne hovered over them with sundry sympathetic tales of all the dreadful things 'them felleys at the railway' had done in their time, even to losing—her voice fell to an awed whisper—' the dacent corpse ov me cousin Timothy Delaney, as dacent a man as iver stthepped. An 'the gran' hearse waitin' on above at the station, two mourning coaches, no less; for me a'nt was bringin' the corpse down to lie wid its own people. An' wasn't the whishky an' ivrythin' there, an' all? but they sint him asthray at the junction, an' disgraced him entirely. So he was buried without a proper funeral next day, dacent man that he was—God rest his soul!'

With all this, it was no wonder that nightmares attended their dreams. They dreamt of horses, maimed or mutilated, travelling in company with the dacent corpse of Timothy Delaney.

But the morrow brought relief. The horses actually arrived, sent on from the racing stable whither they had been sent, and the old mare was returned. The railway people remarked that it was certainly awkward, and that doubtless some foolish porter had affixed the wrong labels in Dublin. That was all their apology.

Then three days passed. Merrylass, who was a little stiff after her journey, was taken out to look at the Irish fences. There was no time to school her before the first meet was upon them, the card announcing, 'Monday, October 30, Georgestown.' It was only a few miles from the town, but Maddigan more or less implied that if they rode out he would be lost to them as a friend.

Brown had an animated time on this first hunting morning, while Hannah Anne completely lost her head, and hovered round them discussing their beauty.

'She had niver,' she said, 'seen the red so adjacent before, an' 'twas nate entirely. The shame it was, indade, to be dirtin' thim fine things, thrapesin' round the country afther a pack ov mad dogs! Slashin' yerselves wid mud, an' wettin' thim lovely boots. 'Twould be fitther for ye, now, to sthay above in the cyar for the day an' show yerselves, clane as ye are now.'

It was clear that Hannah Anne thought their only reason for going out hunting was to air their fine clothes. She greatly approved of their aprons, which, she said, none of the Cahirvally men rode in. 'An' which musht look nate entirely, flappin' above on a horse, besides kapin' thim darlin' breeches clane from the mud.'

If they sent her out of the room, she returned in a second, full of admiration. She entreated the Boy, as she handed him an egg, to 'be careful, now, an' not to dhrop the yally on his clane vesht. ' She reduced Kane-Norton to madness by suddenly dropping on her knees and blowing on his boot, 'becaise a tashte ov salt had fallen on it an' destryed the polish.' Lastly, she nearly wept over Travers because his coat was not a new one. The last they saw of her was waving ' safe-homes ' and 'success' from the doorstep, wringing Brown's hand in her excitement; as a rule she regarded him as a deadly enemy.

They were early for the meet, Maddigan sending the gray mare along past everyone. As they neared the fixture they overtook their horses and he pulled up. Travers gave a sigh of satisfaction as he passed his mare.

'Perfection!' he muttered ecstatically. 'What's that about banks? You know I had her out over some on Saturday, and she put her legs on 'em.'

The Boy remarked that she had brushed one, by chance, with her off hind.

Kane-Norton had brought out his four-yearold, and very well the bay looked now that he was out of his coat and trimmed up, justifying his owner's judgment. He and Merrylass made a splendid-looking pair, but the effect was somewhat marred by the Boy's Ould Tim hopping along on three legs by the big colt's side; Merrylass, needless to say, was too proud to lead.

'I do wish you'd a better mount, Boy,' observed Travers kindly. 'Your brute's lame all round, and only a pony.'

'What '11 you bet,' said the Boy rashly,' that, if we have a hunt, I'm not in front of your flier?' Don't want to steal your money,' said Travers, his eyes on Merrylass's perfect shoulders, her galloping quarters.

'Bet you a fiver,' said the Boy. 'I'm all for faith in Casey.'

The car turned in at a gateway, and the grooms jumped off, polishing up their horses. Merrylass and Tim stood side by side—the mare faultless, sound; Tim hanging his head dejectedly, tottering on his fore-legs, resting the off hind, which was the worst he possessed, but with his lean little head looking round for hounds.

'I'll take you, then,' said Travers. 'I want" a new saddle; you want sitting on. Goodmornin'! Mornin'!'—answering several greetings. 'By Jove! I'm beginning to be awfully glad that we came here. One can see the people mean to be civil. They know we mean real sport. Donovan Moore, now, they call him surly—I can't see it; and little Dick Doyle's the best of fellows.'

Travers was at peace with all the world that morning. It was a soft gray day, light clouds moving with a west wind. It is a sour heart that does not rejoice on the day of the opening meet, when all the winter lies before one, with its hopes of great gallops to be ridden, great deeds to be done. Fresh horses kicked and squealed, cantering past them; traps tore up: men stamped up and down, talking cheerily. They moved off soon, going down a narrow lane.

Ould Tim soon worked sound; he trotted along gaily, snatching at his snaffle-bit. The Boy's heart thumped with excitement. It was his third day's hunting in his whole life; fences were all alike to him; he knew no danger— none of the qualms of doubt which experience teaches. The old horse's perfect shoulders made him a delightful mount.

Leaving the lane, they went into a field, and saw the covert in front—a low patch of gorse, green against a background of sombre firs.

Eager, watching, the pack grouped round Sir Ralph. Then a wave, a word, and the dappled mass flew over the low stone wall, a few stones rattling down under their feet.

'Well, you like this?' Miss Maguire rode up to them, and the Boy looked round at her.

Like it? It was the Promised Land, reaching far away on every side. Grass and grass, and grass again, till it was lost in the purple of the distant hills. Clifford, their tempter, stood close by, riding a neat gray with fired hocks, and a general look of going about him.

Miss Maguire smiled at them, casting a critical eye over the horses. 'Nice, very nice,' she said to Merrylass—' quite above our class here. Your bay is a useful-looking youngster, too '—this to Kane-Norton; 'I seem to know him. ' She passed the Boy by in silent scorn, with a faint smile at Ould Tim.

The men sat straighten Travers patted his mare's neck. They stared round the field; the Cahirvally men might mean going, but poverty handicapped them, and they did not err on the side of smartness. They sold their best horses, and most of those they rode were in the 'coming-on' stage. Travers and Kane-Norton knew they were perfectly turned out, and a thought, sudden—as such thoughts often are— shot through their brains. Grass, all grass, a perfect hunting country, and—an heiress; the rest is not hard to imagine. They were not vain men, but they knew themselves to be different to the sons of the soil, and— newness appeals. The heiress looked at the covert, Kane-Norton screwed in his eyeglass, Travers stroked his upper lip. Miss Maguire spoke suddenly to the Boy, who had never looked away from the gorse, the fleeting vision of pied heads and waving sterns.

'Blank!' she said. 'No use; it's a small gorse. The making of a sportsman/ she added, half to herself.

Blank it was. A note on the horn, the saddest it ever sounds; hounds coming languidly out of covert, rolling on the grass, with disappointed faces. Then away to a gorse on the hillside (Travers rode up with Miss Maguire), where misfortune again awaited them, a fox being headed and chopped.

The third time was the charm. They drew a low-lying gorse, and hounds were scarcely in before a yell announced that their fox was away. Then what a rush and a scramble for the only way out over a big bank, with a drop into the field beyond! Merrylass came fighting down at it, battered into the crowd, and was obliged to walk because there was no room to fly. Kane-Norton was crossed by a smiling lady in an ill-fitting habit, and his eyeglass promptly fell out.

'Give 'em time!' yelled the master.

Hounds flashed out of covert on a burning scent, with a burst of soul-stirring music. Then away on the line, bristles up, close on their fox. Down the field, straight at a big bank, the rush dwindled; the leaders stood out from the crowd. Dick Doyle put his gray at the bank, and Travers, hemmed in on the right, came behind. He thought he allowed his leader heaps of time, but he forgot the prop on the bank, and —Merrylass. Doyle's gray had just got his hind-legs under him, when there was a rush, a bang, and Merrylass soared from field to field, sending the Irish horse staggering out on his head.

'I say, sir, you might have killed me!' Doyle lifted his red head from the gray's mane, whither the bump had sent it. 'What the dickens do you mean by coming here and riding over me? There were places enough in the fence, surely!'

'And I thought they'd excuse us,' murmured Travers, as he shrieked apologies and sawed at his mare's mouth.

Hounds swung to the left across a road, Merrylass changing legs in the centre and flying a yawning ditch on the far side. Agitated country people yelled that 'he was foreninst thim out, facin' Redhill, an' goin' like the winds of hivin!'

The pace in the closely-fenced country was fast enough for anything. Travers sawed at his mare's mouth, but the sound turf beneath her hoofs excited her unduly. She faced her fences with cocked, eager ears, but— she laid no hoof to anything. Travers had strange visions of two ditches flanking the green fences. He felt there were moments when nothing but Merrylass's extraordinary activity saved them from a rattling fall. He sawed at the curb, and the mare began to lose her temper and fling her head about wildly.

A stone wall rose in front of them; it was double, and the only way out of an awkward corner, but he recognised a fly, and was thankful.

A couple of horses jumped in front of him, going on and off the loose stones, and sending a noisy shower down beneath their feet. A shower of these stones rolled into Merrylass's face, frightening her; she flung out her fore-legs with a sullen jerk, and refused.

Just at that moment the Boy came up, charged the wall, which Ould Tim charged on leisurely, and flung back a fresh rattle of stones. He screamed out something concerning a fiver, and was gone. His limbs worked wildly as he went; no one could say that he did not try to help his horse. His legs flew wide at every jump, his hands were in many places; but the old horse, who 'had cared a drunkard,' 'cared ' him, hitching him back when he fell out on his neck, taking no notice of strange tugs at his bridle. Travers urged Merrylass to jump; she only backed and sidled.

'Here, some of you men, get the gentleman's horse over 1' shouted another voice. 'She doesn't like the sound of the stones.' Miss Maguire passed him, sitting very squarely on her big black horse. As if by magic, three men appeared by the fence. The corner was big, and most of the field were jumping a low bank further down.

'Slash her over, yer honour! Give her sthick, the decaiver!'

Travers raised his whip, and was rewarded by a sullen kick. He wore no spurs.

'There's timper for ye, now! Wait a minute; we'll do her. Here, rattle yer hat at her, Mikey!' They tore some sticks from the hedge. 'Now give it to her! Go over, ye divil, ye!' And, ere Travers had half realized what they were doing, or could speak, there was a weird rattle of stones in a hat, followed by a sounding whack across those shining quarters in which flowed the blood of the kings of the turf.

'For God's sake, *stop f* he shouted.

But he did not know the Irish. 'Sthop, is it? An' ye losin' the hunt! Now, Mikey, she's goin': now wid the hat! There for ye—whack! hurroo 1 Be the powers, she's goin'! Success! Begor! Well over!'—as Merrylass launched her maddened self into mid-air and cleared the broken-down wall.

'That'll hearten her,' yelled friendly voices behind.

It was probable it would. Merrylass fled like the wind up the field, her tail tucked down between her strong quar-ters, her ears flat to her head, two weals standing out on her bay coat. Travers saw hounds in front, and took a short-cut, the ' heartening' process making the mare wilder than ever as she took her banks.

Far ahead he could see the Boy, foremost in the chase, hard at work on his patient horse.

'He'll do me,' muttered Travers, 'and— what an exhibition of our riding! The Boy going like one of Mrs. O'Neill's untrussed chickens, I knocking Doyle down, KaneNorton 'He looked round, he looked in front—there was no Kane-Norton; he looked behind — could that someone far in the distance, coming at a walk, be Kane-Norton? It was very like him....

A low bank fenced the field he was in; hounds crossed it lower down. Travers put Merrylass at it, trying to steady her, vainly; she stood well away from the fence, and rose. He saw silver beneath him; there came a roar in his ears, a sensation of cold darkness. The waters closed over his head. He had jumped into a deep pond. Panting, gasping, he clung to the saddle, and was towed to the mud where land began. As he stood up, wiping duckweed from his eyes and face, there was another disturbance of the waters as a chestnut horse clove them with a mighty splash, only, as he had taken the fence at a slower pace, his rider was above water and could speak.

'Is it mad you are,' yelled Moore savagely (Travers saw that he had embroiled himself with another prominent member of the hunt), 'to lead me into a place like this? I came after you, and you never even held up your hand or'

'Man, I was under water,' expostulated Travers, picking off duckweed. 'I'm a stranger. How was I to know of the sea here?'

'That's the way with you English fellows'— the chestnut came wallowing on to sound land, his rider swearing and snarling: 'you ride mad —never look where you are. Get up, now; the hounds are on.' Grumbling furiously, and dripping as he went, Moore galloped away.

Travers squeezed out a few stones'

weight of water, and tried to mount.

'Praises be to Hivin! what brought ye into Jim Brady's pond?' said a voice beside him. (Irish sympathy was again to the fore.) 'Divil a sowl but a fool iver thries to come this way. Here, I'll take a tashte o' wather off ye. They say the bottom goes sthraight down to hell,' the man went on. 'Cattle is oftin dhrowned within, an' wance they hid a corpse in it, an' he niver was found. The boys say the divil put up a hand for him. Thank ye, yer honour! Ye'll find the dogs in the wood beyant.'

Merrylass was visibly subdued as they cantered on; she even condescended to kick back at a bank. They again picked up hounds, checked this time at the 'wood beyant.'

Travers, shivering and ill-tempered, cast sour looks at the two Cahirvally men, who were standing together, evidently uniting in abusing him. He sent a prayer to a much-enduring heaven to send the line across either timber or water. The Boy did not add to his happiness by coming up to ask excitedly where he had found a river to swim. *He* had seen none. The Boy shone with bliss.

At that moment hounds hit off the line, and —who says the gods do not hear?—right across the wide field stretched a flight of posts and rails, strong and black, and—the gate was locked. Horses were pulled to right and left, but from the crowd came Travers, a loop of duckweed festooned round his hat, a trail of dampness falling in his track. Merrylass was not pulled about now; this was her work; she shortened her stride and bucked over like a deer. Travers flung back a glance at some four feet of strong timber, and—the morning was forgotten.

James Doyle's gray jerked sharply round, his owner growling, came up and laid a wise head on the top rail; he knew he could not iget over. Irish eyes stared bitterly at the rails, and the Englishman cantered on alone with the hounds. But not for long. A voice might have been heard to mutter that he was not going to be done, and Tim, the old horse, was put at the timber. Tim never dreamt of

refusing—a better horseman might even have got him across. As it was, with a loose rein, varied by jabs on the mouth, he caught the top rail with his knees, and turned completely over, but 'on the right side,' remarked the Boy as he extricated himself from the ruins of his first tall hat, dived for his stirrup, and pursued Travers.

Their triumph was short-lived; halfway across the field the pack gathered round the mouth of an unstopped hole, and the gallop was over.

'We'll cry quits for that fiver, I suppose, said the Boy, hammering with his fist, trying to make his topper again resume the semblance of a hat and quit that of a drunken concertina.

The lock of the gate was broken by this time, and the field came galloping up. Dick Doyle, quite forgetting his morning's bad temper, rode up to Travers, praising his mare, and Travers decided not to bear malice.

'You,' said Miss Maguire, in accents of severity, to the Boy—' you'll be killed. Fancy trying to jump that timber on that old horse!'

'But I got there/ answered the Boy placidly.

'You might very easily have got— somewhere else,' said the lady dryly. Travers always declares that she pointed downwards with her whip.

Just then, in the calm of resting horses, and wondering what was to be done next, the tones of a spirited argument broke on their ears.

'A brute—an absolute *brute!* He crossed three fields, and then shut up and walked!' Kane-Norton's voice was raised in anger. He'

The gentler tones of Casey, the horse-coper, could be heard declaring that, 'if the gentleman would only remember, he (Casey) had never wanted him to buy the horse—in fact, had wanted him not to.'

'But he walked—I tell you he *walked* f almost wailed Kane-Norton.

Here Casey observed that they had often been very glad to find the horse able to walk.

'Walked, and left me miles behind everyone!'

'He's a white-hearted baste,' said Casey calmly. 'Sure, ye would have yer own way, thinkin we didn't know the horse's value, an' I couldn't bend ye from buyin' him. Ye saw him jump, and ye knew I would give ye no trial; an' my advice to ye is to sell him on as quick as ye can, for 'tisn't in him to go a hunt. I niver wanted ye to have him."

Oppressed by the truth of this statement, Kane-Norton withdrew, still grumbling and unappeased. He had had a cheery ride, absolutely last of all. The bay had given out after the first mile; he jumped, but he could not gallop. A mile or two had seen the end of him.

Their golden dreams were overcast with darkness as they rode homewards, and told their several experiences.

'What I like/ said the Boy slyly, 'about this country, is the welcome they give to a stranger, especially when you jump on 'em and take 'em into duck-ponds!'

'What I like,' said Travers more happily, 'is a post and rails!'

'Expensive!' said the Boy, examining his hat.

Kane-Norton vented his grievances in a sudden burst of spleen, to the effect that' they'd been a nice lot of fools coming over here and imagining that they'd make money out of horses'— here he smote the bay heavily—' in a place where he supposed everyone watched every horse from the time it was born.' There was nothing about the Irish not knowing a horse until it was trimmed up now. It appeared that a great many people had been acquainted with the character of Casey's four-year-old. Also Kane-Norton declared his full intention of coming out and killing the lady with the smile, who had crossed him twice, in the early happy moments when the bay had cantered. Altogether, it was plain that his mistake weighed on his soul.

Hannah Anne opened the door for them, and eyed them gloomily.

'Desthryed!' she said dramatically—' desthryed! The beautiful red clothes an' the darlin' white breeches, and Mr. Travers back with the Cahir river on his back an' in his boots! How, in the name of God, ye can take plisure in it, whin ye might put on the red, an' hire a cyar an' dhrive round safe an' sound an" clane!'

Travers was ordered to take hot whisky, 'becaise her cousin Tim Delaney, the corpse I towld ye of, lost his life through fallin' into a pond when he was dhrunk, and no whisky adjacent—God rest his sowl! I very kittle in the house is hatin' for yez, so give the bell a wallop whin ye're ready, an' I'll wet the tay. Arrah, Holy Mary! look at the sthate of ye!' —this to the Boy, whom she admired fervently.

She vanished, and they could not reprove her, because she had their interests so much at heart, muttering as she went that ''Twas courtin' disaster, an' flyin' in the face of Providince, to be ruinin' good clothes in that way.'

Later, when the three had consumed a great deal of tea and mounds of hot buttered toast, Travers rose and began to write a letter. Kane-Norton, as if it reminded him of some thing, pulled out a stylographic pen, and also began to write. The Boy smoked in happy peace, his face aglow with content.

'I thought'—Travers laid the letter and a penny on the table; Kane-Norton extracted a stamp from his note-case—' I thought we might perhaps ask someone to tea next week, and that it would be a good thing to have some nice sweets and so on in the house. I fancy Mrs. O'Neill'

Kane-Norton looked at the address which he had written on his own letter.

'I—I believe I've been doing very much the same,' he said, a little blankly.

The name on the envelope was Buzzard.

'Why? How? What woman have you two fellows been asking to tea?' said the Boy, swinging quickly round on them.

They answered together: 'Miss Maguire. On Saturday.' CHAPTER V

A TEA-PARTY AND A NEW HORSE

Cahirvally was quite on the edge of the hunting and for a time Travers thought of moving on to one of the small villages where, he was informed, they would be far more comfortable, and would be in the centre for the meets. Then, on due inquiry, they found it was

possible, if they had spare horses, to train to two other packs from the town; so, after weighing pros and cons carefully, they decided to stay where they were. They had grown accustomed to the ways of No. 8, Connel Street; in strange places stranger ways might be their portions, and those they knew were best. If Hannah Anne was wrapped in grime, her heart was large, and she had taken them to it as if they were friends of years.

The next meet, after the eventful first one, was at Ballinagh, and they heard that a special train would convey them out; the fixture was at the other side of the county. Special trains sound business-like; they felt contented, and on Friday three carefully-sheeted horses were despatched to the station. Kane-Norton fussed a good deal that morning, lest they should be late. He quite declined to take Hannah Anne's advice, which was ' To watch for Misther Doyle makin' up for the station, for they'd niver dare to let the thrain off widout him,' and he watched the clock feverishly. Maddigan drove them up in what Kane-Norton considered sharp time, the Boy a little sulky because he had been flurried over his third egg.

'How the deuce, Nor, do you expect a man to ride hard on no breakfast?' he demanded with some asperity.

The start was, even then, marred by Hannah Anne's rushing after them and thrusting a boiling hot package into the Boy's hands.

'Eggs,' she announced—' hard eggs, to kape the life in ye for the long road. I clane forgot thim, ye were all that excited, an' I whipped 'em up now hot out of the pot.'

'No doubt about that,' observed the Boy, shaking his fingers

There were no other hunting people on the platform when they arrived, no bustle or signs of a hunting-train. The station-master, a peppery-looking man with a pug nose and obtrusive chin, was standing at the entrance, and with some importance Travers asked for guidance.

'Special?' Mr. Clancy glared at him; possibly he remembered the arrival of the brood mare. 'Special? Huntin' ye're

going? Now, is there a special this mornin'? Did they decide on one? I'm not rightly sure. Often they orthers one, and thin counter-orthers it at the last minute. Is there one, now, for sure, this morning?'

Travers gasped. This, with the meet twenty miles away, and no other hope of getting there!

'Wait,' said Clancy, as he noted their fallen faces—' wait. I'll ask Doolan; he's here early, an' he's sure to know.'

Mr. Clancy, it appeared, had been but lately promoted to Cahirvally from a distant Western station where hunting was unknown.

The 'porther,' being better informed tha.; his superior, told them where to start from, and carried their bags for them to the train. It was by this time the hour appointed for the train to start; but the distant platform where they were led to was still littered with horses being boxed. One sheeted beast was gyrating up and down, wavering between the horrors of a station lamp waved at her tail and the horse-box in front. At length, further urged by wild cries of 'Quit it now, Dolly Vardin, ye divil! Go up within there, and don't be houldin' us here till night!' she clattered, snorting, up the steep wooden ascent.

Coated men came strolling up, and some few ladies. Amongst the crowd was a man in shooting kit, with a pair of red setters at his heels. The station-master arrived to see the start and to inform them that they were already 'tin minutes late, but, as Misther Doyle hadn't turned up, there wasn't jhe laste chance of their stharting.' At this moment his eyes fell on the setters, and he perceived a way of airing his importance.

'Whose are thim dogs?' he thundered. 'There's nothin' goes on this thrain but the hunthers.'

The owners of the dogs, who had taken advantage of the early train to get out shooting, looked decidedly embarrassed.

'If thim dogs belong to the huntin' party,' said Mr. Clancy firmly, 'they can go, but if not they must remain in Cahirvally.'

A silence followed while arguments

were being thought out, for they all knew how Clancy delighted in making himself disagreeable.

'Good heavens!' The Boy swung round on the peppery official. 'Don't you know a hound by sight, you people here? These are a new pair going out to Sir Ralph, quite the best hounds he's got, and I shouldn't like to be you if he hasn't got 'em to kill foxes with to-day.'

A couple of sporting porters hid their heads and spluttered convulsively. Then, amid a general subdued titter, Mr. Clancy nodded his head majestically, and remarking that he would take any trouble to oblige Sir Ralph, he put the hounds and their owner into an empty first-class carriage, while to the said owner, whom he knew by sight, he gave many last directions as to the care of the dogs.

At this point Doyle arrived, and they steamed off, some fifteen minutes late, KaneNorton, full of suppressed fury, inclined to glare at everyone, the rest of the people content to trust to Providence, as they had often done before.

The train ran through the grass country, past a stretch of brown bog; then past green slopes wide and desolate, fenced by tattered stone walls. A mist veiled the sky, an eerie stillness hung over the land, the gray wreaths seemed to cling to the thorns on the hedges. They dashed across level crossings, where dirty flags were waved mildly at them, and donkeycarts waited at the wooden gates. There was no stir of life anywhere. It was Ireland —desolate, lonely, yet ever beautiful in her desolation and her loneliness.

A jar, a grating bump—they pulled up at Lismore to pick up some other passengers. The doors were banged again, but they did not go on, and there was some bustle on the platform.

'What's up?'

Travers put his head out of the window and was duly informed that ' Faith, the brakes was sthuck, an' they couldn't git thim off at all, at all.'

Kane-Norton immediately pushed Travers aside, and his head, shaded by a perfectly brushed topper, was thrust out.

'Are we never going on?' he thundered furiously. 'If ever I catch myself coming by one of these rotten trains again!'

By this time there were heads out of every window.

'In a minute, in a minute, yer honour!'a person with a banded cap, who seemed to be in authority, answered. 'Here, Mikey, for the love of Hivin, sthep down off the ingin an' see if ye can kick off thim brakes! They're sthuck below here; I towld thim not to use this train agin, but I suppose they thought 'twould do for the huntsmin. Come on, Mikey! Pat here hasn't the strength of a mouse in him.'

Thus adjured, a smutty head was thrust out of the engine, and the driver came to help the porter, who was kicking wildly at some unseen obstacles on the wheels.

'Good—GoodZ,ord/' observed Kane-Norton, treading heavily on Donovan Moore's toe as: he stepped helplessly backwards. 'What class of thing is this?'

'Mikey, ye're a jewel! Success to yer toe!' said a triumphant voice outside. 'That sames the lasht of thim now. Dhrive her on now like hell, so as to catch the dogs at the mate, an' have an eye on thim brakes—the divil to thim!—for fear they schame on ye agin, an" run ye through Ballinagh widout goin' on for ye.'

With this comfort on their ears they started on again, Donovan glaring furiously and nursing his toe. He had noticed KaneNorton's attentions, and felt he had no cause to love the stranger who had come among them. He and Dick Doyle were running a close race for the heiress. They wanted no fresh entries. The brakes were good to them, and they pulled up at the meet. They were out now in the wildest part of the country. Steep hills towered in front, with a valley fair enough to have attracted any sporting wraith from paradise running below the heights.

Miss Maguire, mounted on a magnificent gray, gave them friendly greeting, and, all ills forgotten, they rode beside her as they climbed the rough winding

road to the covert, while close behind, their faces set grimly, jogged the two thrusters of the hunt, united in their anger, Donovan Moore's harsh drawl mingling with Doyle's quick, sharp tones.

Faultlessly attired, sitting with the long easy seat he prided himself on, clad by the pioneers of hunting fashion from the shining brim of his hat to the shining toe of his boot, and mounted on his handsome short-legged black, with his big plain flapped saddle and heavy, workmanlike-looking double bridle, KaneNorton was distinctly good to look at. Travers was equally well got up, though his pink bore the marks of hard usage. The mare bent her satiny neck to the light touch of the curb, champing at her bit, and stepping as a lady does who is aware of her claims to beauty.

As they reached the top of the hill, Miss Maguire pointed with her whip towards a square white house nestling in woods hazy in the distance.

'Dunmore, my house,' she said. 'I'm right in the centre for hunting. We shoot later. You must come out if you care for it.'

They hastened to assure her that, next to hunting, shooting was the passion of their lives. Then they were silent. The white house looked homelike. All round stretched the dreamland they had come to. Level pasture, open and practically hedgeless; here and there a small smudge of brown plough. Good shooting down there among those thick trees, and away to the right of the house ran a purpling patch of bogland where snipe must abide. They looked again, and then at the big comely girl, her fair hair shining under her small hard hat. Then they looked at each other. For the first time in their lives they were rivals, and rivals for so great a prize. Their actions were characteristic. KaneNorton screwed his eyeglass tighter; Travers patted his mare's neck fondly. Somehow, he trusted to her and her beauty. Behind them the two Cahirvally men in their locally-made coats, on their snaffle-bridle horses, growled almost audibly.

'Have you brought your lunatic out to-day?' asked Miss Maguire suddenly.

Kane-Norton coughed apologetically; he hoped her dislike to the Boy might not influence her against them.

'He's new to the game, he said. 'You mustn't be hard on him; he's a cracked youngster.'

'So,' said Miss Maguire. 'So—a very '— 'cheeky' hovered on her lips—' outspoken youngster. But the makings of a sportsman '— this to herself.

The draw lay along the hill. The valley was veiled in the mist; moisture clung to the straggling thorns, lay silver thick on the lush grass of the big banks. It was a day for a hunt, and a crashing chorus in covert told them a fox was at home. But high hopes soon dropped. The fox made for the valley, but the scent was catchy, uncertain. One minute they were racing along; the next, hounds were hopelessly at fault. And so they dragged on and on, across a perfect country, big and honest. It was one of those hunts in which a man is alternately on top of hounds, getting cursed at by the master, or far behind, as they take a sudden turn away from him. It was at one of these unlucky moments that, having taken his eyes off hounds, Kane-Norton saw them tearing away in front, and he took a short-cut to get to them, grumbling at the uncertainty of the day.

'There's wire that way,' said a melodious voice in his ear.

He turned to see a girl close to him. She rode a slashing roan horse, one that he had remarked more than once during the day, jumping perfectly. He then said that he couldn't see any wire.

'It's hidden in the next fence,' said the girl briefly. 'They're swinging back to covert. I'll show you the shortest way.'

Kane-Norton obeyed, following her. His guide was a small girl with a brilliant complexion and pathetic blue eyes. She wore a badly-fitting habit, and she rode perfectly. She put her horse at a high stone-faced bank, one of the ugliest fences they had jumped for the day. Kane-Norton, whose black blundered a little, admired the perfect way in which she handled the roan, and the equally perfect way in which the horse had changed on the narrow, slippery top. He

expressed his admiration, and the stranger turned her pathetic eyes upon him, and told him that it was the best horse she had ever owned, yet she was obliged by hard fate to sell it. Here she met his eyes with a glance of pure pathos, so perfect as to give some hint of practice. Kane-Norton felt his well-regulated English heart giving way.

'Mr. Doyle's after it,' she said in her low voice as they trotted on easily, for the hounds had checked again, 'and the Caseys wanted it for some stranger.'

Kane-Norton pricked his ears. He had commissioned the Caseys to buy him something good.

But Doyle never would give a price,' she went on, 'and, of course, Casey would want his profit.'

He began to grow eager. They crossed a wide stream, a built wall, and a big double (whenever he saw a gap his guide had some excellent reason for not going that way), and all the time the little stream of confidences trickled into his ear. He began to think. Why not buy the horse direct and save Casey's profits? He hinted something, and was surprised to find how quickly he drifted into a deal.

'There's only one thing,' said the blue-eyed girl as they reached the others. 'You'll promise me to be kind to my Paddy;' and her blue eyes looked so childlike and melting that KaneNorton wanted to take her into his arms and comfort her. 'You might as well take him home this evening,' added the little girl, seemingly as an afterthought. 'I'll take him to the train for you.'

Full of pride, Kane-Norton rode up to Miss Maguire to tell her of his new purchase. He pointed it out as the girl rode away down the field.

'I never saw such a lepper as that was,' he said, 'and I saw it gallop, too. The girl's a wonderful child to ride as she does.'

Miss Maguire took out some sandwiches, and bit one leisurely.

'It's a splendid jumper,' she said. 'She had it part of last year. A very good-looking horse. How much are you giving?'

Kane-Norton named the price.

'And worth all that.' Kane-Norton felt himself puffing like the fabled frog. 'When he passes the vet, he'll be worth all that and more.'

'Good heavens!' said Kane-Norton. 'Do you know, I quite forgot about the vet. I thought that a lady—she'd be sure to'

'Well, think of it now,' said Miss Maguire dryly. 'That innocent little monkey is one of the biggest horse-copers in the country, and has forgotten more about a horse than you ever knew. ' (Was it Doyle who chuckled hoarsely?) 'She's had her eye on you all day, and probably followed you down there. I've no pity for her. Take my advice: don't appear to know anything, but say you will send Morgan out on Thursday to vet the horse.'

'Great heavens!' said Kane-Norton, 'have I come to this country simply to be stuck.'

He never got the slashing roan. The pathetic young lady wrote to say that she had changed her mind, and would not sell her horse that season. Moreover, she bore no malice, nor ever mentioned the subject again, but took it as a friendly introduction, and used her blue eyes upon Kane-Norton every time she met him.

The gray day ended uneventfully. The Boy, with the taste for low society which they were beginning, with pain, to notice, spent his spare moments with the Casey brothers. He bestowed a passing smile on Miss Maguire, who seemed inclined to speak to him, but he rode past, deep in a whisky-scented conversation with James Casey.

Travers and Kane-Norton spent most of the day with the heiress, always with a grumbling, uneasy pair somewhere in the background. They finished by partaking of a heavy tea at the village of Lismore, and then steaming back to Cahirvally in a leisurely manner.

In the crowded days which followed they made many acquaintances. Whispers were muttered round as to their long incomes, their state of bachelordom, and cards lay in heaps on the round table. These callers generally arrived during their absence, and the cards were mixed in a cheery fashion by Hannah Anne, who sorted them with running comments as to the status of their visitors.

They returned visits feverishly, and all might have gone well with them if, in a spirit of economy, brought on by finding what it cost them to hunt, they had not dispensed with Maddigan's services, and sallied forth lightheartedly to exercise their horses and call at the same time. The great clan of Doyles confused them. They inquired sweetly at the first house they went to, a long, straggling building with the plaster peeling from the walls, for Mrs. Peter Doyle, who, it turned out, had been buried a short month before. After one swift glance of amazement, the Irish maiden's natural politeness came to her rescue, and she informed them that 'if 'twas Mrs. Pether's grave they were wishful to see, and had come about that, 'twas quite convanient down the dhrive, where all the family was buried, and, indade, the flowers was hardly withered yet above on it.'

They fled hastily, speeding to other Doyles. Needless to say, the sorrowing widower had never called on them at all.

But they did better at the next place by asking for Mr. Doyle where the owner bore the title of a Colonel—in the militia—and the maid remarked with much hauteur that 'if 'twas the Colonel they were wanting, he was widin, but if 'twas Misther Doyle they were comin' to see, faith, they'd bether go on to Ballyalla, the second next gate on the right.'

After this they gave up trying to sort the people, and left it to the Boy, who made matters quite safe by cheerily demanding in the language of the country 'if there was anyone within,' which remark, delivered in a superfine English, had an excellent effect.

They met the four Miss Clancys, buxom red-headed girls who lived in a big house on the borders of the town, and hovered also on the borders of society. Claheen was a merry house where a man might spend Sunday afternoon bathed in a cloud of tobacco-smoke, and

surrounded by empty soda-water bottles; the whisky decanters stood, always ready, on the table. This atmosphere was pleasantly varied by walks taken with one of the Miss Clancys— to the very end Travers never quite sorted them—to see the dogs or the horses, or to admire the flowers in the big unkempt garden.

During these walks the Englishmen learnt many phases of the fine art of flirtation, which had hitherto been hidden from them, and it is doubtful if any of them—with the exception of the Boy, who could generally rise level with the occasion—came up to the mark required. The two elder Miss Clancys, it appeared, possessed aspirations to culture and the latest fashion. They studied the papers to see how the world moved, and tea, served in the very latest method advised by the ladies' weeklies, mingled with the soda-water and the whisky. They were asked to dine there later, but that tale comes by itself.

Amongst all this rush, the owners of the few large places in the county failed to honour them with a visit, and Kane-Norton was duly aggrieved. The Boy declared that it was only his influence which prevented the elder man from forwarding their respective pedigrees— on postcards—to the leading lights of Cahirvally. But the Boy was prone to exaggeration. So the days slipped by, until Miss Maguire, who had put them off once, settled a day on which to come to tea. When that day came, Hannah Anne's patience was worn thin. New teacups were hired; a new tea-cloth was bought, to hide the tea-tray. This cloth was of so fine a quality that the stout damsel almost struck at using it, and put forward a wish to convert it into ''macassars' for the dirty chairs. They had provided sweets and many cakes, and Mrs. O'Neill promised them griddle-cakes of supreme excellence. The Boy retreated himself on that busy morning, none knew where; ibut, as Miss Maguire never appeared to like 'him, they were rather pleased at his absence.

At about four-thirty the lady, accompanied by a cousin as chaperon, strolled

in. The big girl looked so well in her perfectly-fitting gray tailor-made, with a high white collar, and a hard sailor hat on her fair hair, that the game took a step forward and grew serious. If Miss Maguire lived in plough-land, and owned no farthing of her own, she was still well worth the winning.

With a glance round the room and a careless remark that it was cleaner than when she had seen it last, Miss Maguire sat down, and, in response to a peal on the bell, Hannah Anne came clumping up with tea.

But, alas for their preparations! A duster, to which cleanliness was long a stranger, guarded the snowy cloth, and the largest kitchen teapot reposed on the tray. In response to a spirited and audible aside from Kane-Norton, Hannah Anne returned heatedly that she 'couldn't have it on her sowl to be sphillin' tay on the likes of that dandy cloth, and that, sure, the little chancy taypot that they was after buyin' jumped out of her hand and was in three bits on the flure below —bad manners to thim bits of things! An', sure, the tay would be twice as nice out of a fine warrm pot. ' Here Miss Maguire giggled helplessly, and Kane-Norton wiped a furious brow and gave it up.

Hannah Anne was incorrigible; it was impossible to snub or remove her. She appeared with relays of smoking cakes, and herself invited the ladies to partake, which they did, with a shameless disregard for their digestions.

Her nose appeared round the door again and again, and it was only when cigarettes were produced, and Miss Maguire took one, that Hannah removed the tea-things with a clatter, her nose well in the air, and retreated to her bosom friends in the little shop at the corner of the street to enlarge to them on the shamelessness of the quality ladies, 'puffin' shmoke like steam-ingins above, and ne'er a soul but themselves to care them."

The conversation did not flag; they found plenty to talk of. Travers sat close to Sheila Maguire; Kane-Norton leant against the chimneypiece. The cousin, a quiet girl of about twenty, was, if not quite neglected, a little left on one side. Kane-Norton was rather inclined at all times to make himself the central figure— to hold forth, as it were. The conversation slipped round to their respective races, and this was a subject on which he considered himself more than qualified to give an opinion.

'What I object to in you Irish,' said KaneNorton grandly, 'is your — well, democratic tendency. You mix, you speak to the lower classes, in a way which no English person would think of doing.'

'No harm in that,' observed Miss Maguire, looking at him narrowly.

'No harm exactly, but it rather destroys the distinctive distance of class from class.'

'Perhaps so,' said Miss Maguire thoughtfully.

There was a clatter of hoofs in the street below; Miss Maguire looked out of the window.

'You can see that,' pursued Kane-Norton.

'See? Oh, I see what you mean 1' she said over her shoulder.

'Hannah Anne! Hannah Anne! Hang you, Hannah Anne! where are you?' said the Boy's voice on the stairs. 'Come up a bit, then— *they* must get it. Here, you fellows, bring out the whisky to me!' The Boy flung open the door. He was somewhat dishevelled; his hat was on one side, his boots were very muddy, and he clutched by the arm a grinning farmer, who strove bashfully to back away. A faint reek of fiery whisky bore down the breeze. 'Oh, how'd ye do? Excuse me, Miss Maguire, but I've bought this man's horse, and I had to bring him back here to pay him, and I must give him a drink, ye know, and there's no other room. Give me the decanter, you two.'

He shut the door, filling a brimming beaker as he went.

Travers breathed again as the door closed, but Miss Maguire, after another glance into the street, got up and opened it.

'I see the horse down there,' she said; 'I'd like to look at him.'

'Come on, James,' said the Boy.

'We'll show the lady the horse.'

And then Kane-Norton felt the shame of it tingling down his backbone as the Boy preceded Miss Maguire, and went arm-in-arm— yes, arm-in-arm—with the dirty farmer down the stairs, one friendly hand stretched backwards to encourage the lady to follow, and— she followed quite calmly.

The Boy babbled excitedly as he went: the man stumbled a little once; clearly the last glass of whisky had been potent. The cousin and the two men— both the latter very angry— came downwards also. The Boy's voice rang clearly up to them. His sentences were muddled:

'Casey told me of this fellow—good fellow, Casey!—an' so I went out to-day to try him and so on; and I'd have been back long ago, but I knew the value, and this ruffian here kept me all day getting the last two quid off.' He shook the man's arm. Kane-Norton paused, dumb from horror; Miss Maguire nodded approvingly. 'Then we had to drink to the bargain, y' see'—the Boy made wry faces at this memory—'and I made him bring the horse straight in to be vetted, and here we are.'

They surged out the hall door. Hannah Anne, on seeing them, bolted back from her shop and went into the hall behind them. The horse, a big gray, held at the moment by a small gamin, and the ever-patient Ould Tim, held by no one, stood at the door. The new purchase was a fine upstanding colt, with great bone and substance, galloping quarters, and undeniable shoulders. The sole crab, the Boy told them, was a chip out of one knee.

He danced round his new purchase— the Boy was always excitable—but a horrible suspicion began to dawn on his friends. Was it all due to excitement at the present moment, or had that potent whisky, combined with the fresh air, been too much for him? What an ending it was to their carefully-planned tea-party! Miss Maguire seemed kind enough to overlook things; she passed over the Boy's wild manner, and walked round and round, scanning the horse carefully. Then she asked how he was bred.

'I thought so!' she cried as they told her. 'He's a half-brother of my good grays; I saw the likeness at once.'

Now, what was there in this speech to make the Boy slap Miss Maguire enthusiastically on the back with one hand, while with the other he banged the horse's late owner. Miss Maguire jumped at the friendly bang, and Kane-Norton, too weak to bear more, leant helplessly against the iron railings. His support was soon reft from him; Hannah Anne came with a shrieking skirl from the house, crying that 'them railings was rotten, an' only tied together wid sthring!' The violence of the drag brought him panting against the damsel's plump bosom, and one of his feet slipping down the steps, thither he remained for a space, his arms about her neck, unable to regain voice or balance. Hannah Anne held him bravely. Travers and the cousin quite unable to overcome their laughter, sat down together on the grimy steps and indulged it loudly; while a couple of passing carters, without precisely knowing what they were laughing at, stopped and joined in, just to be friendly. It was at this moment that Miss Maguire, who had had her back to the doorsteps, elected to turn and take her leave.

Kane-Norton raised a ruffled yellow head from the dirty check blouse it reposed on, and grasped at his dignity and his balance. His eyeglass, needless to say, was floating on the breeze.

The Boy was moving off with his purchase, but the youngster, not being accustomed to town life, shied violently at the selection of saddlery hung outside the little shop opposite, and backed snorting. The late owner came in the rear, mingling curses with thick-voiced fears of losing his train home.

The Boy in turn cursed him for not getting the horse past, and assured him that, if the train were missed, Hannah Anne would put him up, which sounded doubtful.

Ould Tim, clearly bored, followed, led by the gamin.

'Good-bye/ said Miss Maguire, holding out her well-shaped brown hand. 'Good-bye. Thank you so much for my enjoyable tea. It's been quite delightful, especially the horsedealing part. That's a really nice youngster, and bred like my own. There are moments, I imagine' — she spoke to Kane-Norton— 'when even Englishmen seem to mingle quite happily with the lower orders—er— when— buying horses—and—on doorsteps. *Good-bye!*' 'Good-bye, Mr. Rivers,' she called to the struggling Boy.

'Good-bye,' said the Boy carelessly. 'Oh, hang this stupid horse!'

'*What* must that girl think of us?' said Kane-Norton limply.

'I don't know,' said Travers, following a gray-clad figure with his eyes.

'Did—did—she think—that—I—fell against that woman—on—purpose?' demanded KaneNorton in staccato tones.

'One never knows what the Irish may think,' said Travers, wiping some loose dirt, collected on the steps, from his best tweed trousers.

'The Boy—the Boy was undoubtedly—well, not sober'

'Merely confused from country whisky and excitement on an empty stomach. Put it that way. Principally excitement The Boy never drinks.'

'Miss Maguire will never come near us again. And as for that creature Hannah '—he glanced balefully towards the corner whither his muffled curses had banished Hannah Anne—' I declare I will come to an understanding. I will inform Mrs. O'Neill that it's past bearing'

From the corner came a well-known voice, high above the noises of the street:

'An' if it 'twasn't for me, that fine lodger we have, with the glass stuck continuous in his eye, would be dead below on the airey flags. A wakeness he seemed to git, sudden-like, and I, be the marcy of Hivin, seein' him stagger and dipind for support on the bit of ould sthring I took off Doolan's sthone of inyins lasht week, for the railing is clean split in the middle—an' I, as I was sayin', seein' him, I runs out and took a-howld of him, and says I'

'Oh, damn *all* these Irish 1' said KaneN orton, retreating and banging the door behind him.

CHAPTER VI HOW KANE-NORTON BE-CAME A POLITICIAN

When Kane-Norton had first arrived at Cahirvally, he had felt hurt and injured because the lords of the soil—Lord Cahir, better known in Cahirvally as the Earl; Lord Ballyhale; and other people of that ilk—had not made his acquaintance.

He was a particular man; he foresaw that on his return to England he might be questioned as to whom he had known during the winter, and it seemed a shameful thing to him to have to head his list with Doyles and bring it up with Clancys. 'The Cahirs. They're always over for the winter: of course you met them?' Kane-Norton felt uncomfortable in anticipation. Somewhere deep in his soul was a substratum of snobbishness, which he designated 'being particular.' He thought of the roll of his relations, and he pondered deeply on his present situation. He cast glances at the imposing front of Cahir Castle, and wondered why he had not the right to pass behind the portals.

The Knox girls hunted regularly, and he knew that it was a sacred duty with the Cahirvally men to make way for them on all occasions. He himself had altered his course more than once to open gates, to clear gaps for the girls on their thoroughbreds, and had been rewarded by friendly glances from good-tempered freckled faces. He progressed no further.

But at last fortune and a hunting lunch at Cahir Castle favoured him. A mutual friend was staying there; Kane-Norton was formally introduced to Lady Cahir, and was able to unbosom himself of the fact that their friends were his friends, their people his people.

Lady Cahir, a pretty faded woman, who had never outgrown the idea that all the Irish country people were a species of half-tamed wild beast, clad by some godly authority in human skins, distinctly received a chill when she found that he actually lodged in the town of Cahirvally—so much so that Kane-Norton went to much trouble to explain that they did not have earthen floors and turf fires, and that Mrs. O'Neill gave them something to eat besides potatoes. Her ladyship, it appeared, during their twenty years of married life, had driven three times through Cahirvally, and that was her sole acquaintance with it. She had not an Irish servant in the house.

He proceeded to introduce the Boy, but that youth was in a hurry to mount, and disappeared with a careless word. Still, Kane-Norton felt languidly—as he felt most things—that he was being recognised. He accepted an invitation to shoot, and returned that evening full of chastened joy—full also of pity, which was not devoid of irritating patronage, because he had not been able to introduce the other two or receive invitations for them, the Boy especially, with his relations of many heraldries. But the Boy was hopeless. He remarked that he'd much rather shoot with Mickey than kill tame pheasants, and eat Martin's soda loaves than any shooting lunch. He warned KaneNorton at his peril not to introduce his name,' lest he should be asked there and have to play cards, and thus lose money. Kane-Norton took this for a little natural pique, and smiled loftily.

There was, therefore, a faint sense of friction when they fell to talking of the day, of the good country they had ridden over, the many fences they had crossed. It died out after a minute.

'Blessed be the day that sent us here!' said Travers heartily, poking the fire with his toe, 'and the Caseys who have sold us horses!' On hunting nights they generally trusted to Mrs. O'Neill's cookery, and ate game or chickens. Cahirvally meat, prepared by their landlady, was beyond them.

'Blessed be the cousin who has now gone away and deserted us!' said Kane-Norton.

'Here's Hannah Anne,' said the Boy hungrily.

Hannah Anne banged the door open with her large tray, and entered, bearing eight steaming plover on a china dish. The birds were plump, underdone—it was Mrs. O'Neill's one certainty—and they ate them, with a shameless disregard of custom, in company with floury brown-skinned potatoes—which, Hannah Anne had taught them, with a 'taste of salt butther,' were the best thing in life with game. They topped up with apple pie, sardines, and cheese, and then sat over the fire, six slippered feet above the grate, with the happiness of men who know not indigestion. A day in the open air, a happy sense of fatigue which is not exhaustion, further aided by plover and potatoes, promotes dreaminess. As the smoke gathered in a sulphury haze, silence fell on them—they dreamt dreams.

Travers thought of a certain square white house out among the woods. Once he had dreamt of it because it was the key to the Promised Land, because the girl to whom it belonged held her place in the grass country. Now love tinged his dream — his mouth softened. There was something so fresh, so taking, about the tall girl, with her wonderfully fine skin and somewhat bullying manner. If success lay with him, this trip would indeed have been a happy one. He looked at Kane-Norton's languid handsome face and sighed.

Kane-Norton's dreams were not so much of love to-night. There had been many moments in Cahirvally when he had been bored. Now, after to-day, he would move again among the people he belonged to; play bridge after dinner for decent points, instead of spoil-five with Mr. Clancy for pence (Kane-Norton invariably lost); talk the clipped, careless tongue which he understood best; hear little scandalous tales of absent friends.

The Boy's dreams were of horse, and horse alone — memories of the lift Ould Tim had given him to his active quarters as they cleared a big wall; the clever change the old horse had made on a rotten bank; memories of the joy of the chase to one who is absolutely without fear, and who does not know a bad fence from a good one. He thought of his new gray, a horse bold as a lion, but whose jumping was sketchy and given to ending in blunders. Hunting— there was nothing like it, thought the Boy, varied in due course by fishing and shooting. The joys of intellectual pur-

suits did not belong to him. He read the sporting column in a paper, and the war news, if there was any, then he felt his duty was over. He could chuckle over Jorrocks or Soapy Sponge, but the ordinary novel was no pleasure to him.

Then, with all these happy memories quicken, ing his blood, the Boy looked into the firesighing, for none of the sports he loved were assured to him. He was spending his capital, and the day loomed ever nearer when he must go forth into the world and work a little.

Some coals fell with a crash, rousing them. Hannah Anne came in with a kettle to make their nightly supply of punch. She was not in the best of spirits, and remarked that 'the missus had the head whipped off her, because the thray had med one lep out of her hand on to the kitchen flure, an' every taste of chancy was in ribbons. Indade an' indade, she niver saw the missus so fairly cross in her timper. An' 'twasn't much *she* iver broke, only an odd bit of a thing that, to sphite her, would sthrike the flags.'

They thought of the clatter of china which came from the kitchen, and wondered how anything remained whole, or how Mrs. O'Neill's patience ever lasted. But Hannah Anne in her way was invaluable. She did two servants' work, brushing dirt from visible spots into corners where it remained in heaps; dusting the side of ornaments facing the room; blackening grates lustily, and then wiping grimy hands on her apron as she rushed out to bring up breakfast, the plates suffering a final rub from the said apron. But she was always cheerful, always ready to run messages, to hold horses, to do anything which was not her own work. Brown had long ago abandoned the unequal contest and submitted meekly. He arranged rooms and answered doors, while Hannah Anne laid out the men's hunting clothes.

If there was one thing above another which the plump damsel loved, it was to get to a theatre. She often spoke of it— ' not them gran' things where there was just gintlemin an' ladies walkin' about an' talkin' as any real crayture might do,' but the melodrama as played in the

dirty booths which cropped up on the market-field, near the edge of the river.

Once she met Travers and Kane-Norton in the straggling street by the old gray bridge and pointed out the tent to them, suggesting that, if they wanted amusement, they should come, too. There was every preparation made for 'the quality,' she informed them: 'Two rows o benches with red cloth laid on thim, an' a fine tashte of sawdust to kape the wet from the feet.' Touched with some slight curiosity, they came near the grimy wheeled house, and saw the grimier haggard players peering at them. The prices were marked on a bill at the entrance. Kane-Norton put up his eyeglass, then dropped it. 'Boxes, 4d.; Circle, 3d.; Pit, id.' Above was a legend written in large letters: 'No Ladies With Bare Feet Allowed In The Boxes.'

Observing this, Kane-Norton left hurriedly, throwing horrified glances behind him, Hannah Anne's encomiums of the play, her anxiety that they should participate in her pleasure, ringing in his ears.

The wide dingy quay had once been the fashionable quarter of the town. Tall houses glanced down at the unclean river—sad old houses thinking of the day when the river had run cleanly to the sea brown and sweet, to fight the muddy, sullen tide which met it as it did now; of the day when coaches had stood at their doors, when gay ladies and brave men had tripped down their oaken stairways, and gutter children, ragged poverty, had been unknown to them.

Next morning, after a visit to their horses, they went out for a walk, a promise to take tea with Miss Clancy chaining the Boy to the town for the afternoon. They struck out across the country with the happy certainty that, wherever they went, no man would turn them off.

On their way back Kane-Norton bored them a little by talking of his new acquaintances. He was one of those men who know everyone's history, and Lady Cahir's was now reeled off for them. She was of the old-fashioned type, he told them, of the golden race of aristocrats which were vanishing so rapidly—

a lady who, judged by appearances, had little patience with the new race which was springing up. It was evident that he did not fear her judgment of him.

The round they had taken led them homewards through the dirtier, older part of the town, under the shadow of the great cathedral which had sprung up, like some towering fungus, among the shabby houses, its tapering spire nosing far into the sky. In the open square before the church their way was blocked by a mighty crowd, odorous, noisy, green banners, wrought with strange devices, tottering in its depths. It was evident that they had encountered some political meeting of a monster nature. Packed in the crowd they saw a landau, which held two self-important, badly-dressed men, who as they came up were haranguing the multitude in the cheap, flat, town-bred Irish which is more aggravating than any brogue. The speech, with a last sweep of a black-coated arm, cama to an end, to be caught up on a wave of uneven hoarse yelling; hats darkened the air, the green banners trembled. England the conqueror, the hated tyrant, was cursed by hundreds of enthusiastic throats. The mass of people swayed towards the landau; for the moment the stumpy little man it held was a god to them. He, on his part, bowed, smiled, and took a voice lozenge. He was paid to be violent, but it was slightly exhausting.

Kane-Norton stiffened his neck, the blood of the dominant race rising. They looked at other streets, but the only way they knew to take them home was through the crowd, and the lanes and alleys which seemed to lead in the right direction were blocked also.

'Make way there, please,' said Kane-Norton crisply, with the full intention of being obeyed.

Now, the man he happened to speak to was drunk, crossly drunk. The unmistakable Saxon accent, the tone of command, struck rawly.

'Make way? Oh yes, make way for ye—ye English!' he mumbled savagely. He was a huge hulking fellow, well over six feet, with bright blue eyes set in a shrewd-looking face.

Had it been Travers or the Boy, they would have passed on quietly, but they wcre a little behind, listening with much amusement to a pair of old men arguing fiercely as to how they would celebrate the moment when Ireland should be set free. Finally, they both seemed to come round to the idea that a drink was the best way of celebrating anything, and, with a view of finding out if it would serve, they set off to practise for futurity.

'English!' sneered the big man, towering over Kane-Norton.

Kane-Norton flushed. 'Certainly English. Now let us pass, please,' he said stiffly.

'And will we now, will we?' That fiery speech of the M.P.'s was still hot in his muddled mind. 'Will we, wid yer orders?'

A crowd is like a child—easy to interest; it surged together now, applauding the drunken man. 'Dinny Heggarty was the felly to talk to thim. Begob, he was! Listen to the gran" talk of his lordship there! We're to make way for thim always, indade!'

Dinny Heggarty swayed with the pressing mass, a mighty man in his drunkenness. The importance reached his muddled brain; for the moment he was a greater man, doing more for his country, than even Mr. O'Hara, the M.P. They were all listening now to him; he must do something to uphold this country of his.

'Let ye pass?' he rumbled. 'We will—at our own time, whin ye salute our banner there, whin ye say, "God save Ireland! God save Parnell!" If not, ye may go back the way ye came.'

The impotent sense of being the weaker, the knowledge that he was powerless to move these wild, odoriferous patriots, blunted KaneNorton's sense of fitness. Where were the soldiers of the King? Where was England in her might to sweep this mob away before him— an Englishman?

'Salute it! Say "God save Ireland!"' Dinny Heggarty breathed bad whisky and patriotism into his face.

'I'll be damned if I do,' said Kane-Norton crisply. 'Make way there—we

wish to get home.' Though the road to heaven lay bchind him, he would not have taken it now.

'Then, ye may go back, go back /' yelled the drunken giant insolently. 'Go back, ye dirty English!' he leered, secure in his power. 'Ireland's in yer way, an' for wance ye can't pass her out.'

'Get out of my light!' Kane-Norton took a step forward, and the crowd surged together, cheering their spokesman.

'There'll be a lane for ye whin ye sphake the word. Come on now, Englishman!'

Kane-Norton was slow to rouse, but he was no coward. The blood of the dominant race broke bounds; his head went.

'Here you are, then, if I must speak: God save the King f he said in strident tones, his hat in the air. 'Yes, come on if you like,' as Heggarty flung himself forward with a roaring growl.

The air seemed alive with shouts, with clenched fists, as the clear voice cut across the humming brogue of the crowd, as it struck, like match to tow, on the minds still fresh from their M.P.'s hot, salaried vituperation of England— the wicked country which had made them slaves, and without which they would have found it impossible to live

They had never been in a hotter corner; an angry mob is not responsible for its actions.

It was Dinny Heggarty's quarrel first of all. He rushed forward: Kane-Norton struck out, and the big man dropped into a heap of mud, with a bump as big as an egg coming out on his forehead.

'Well sthruck, begob!' cried one of the hottest patriots in the seething mass.

The Boy, backed by Travers, dashed up. They saw the row was on. Their place was by their friend's side. They put their backs against the wall and faced the crowd. Mingled with the hoarse cries of anger, as the Irishmen pressed forward, came the crisp smack of knuckles against flesh, dull thuds as men went down.

It was skill versus strength—strength which could have overcome them at any moment if the crowd had surged in. But after a minute their enemies drew back, comparing wounds, and looking to Dinny for advice. KaneNorton's sense of fitness was merged in a longing for conquest. His tie was gone, his cheek bled from a blow with a stick, his hat was on the ground. The crowd growled and watched them, not too anxious to begin again, for the Boy and Kane-Norton hit like sledge-hammers. The occupants of the landau, having got wind of the fight, were frantically striving to reach them. The 'numbers' wanted no bloodshed, and they knew what the crowd might do. The joy of killing would be too much for them if they got their foes down.

'Come on, you bullies! What about "God save Ireland!" now?' thundered Kane-Norton, his languor a thing of the past. His eyes blazed as he stood facing the crowd, who with one well-timed rush could have trodden them down.

The noise of the carriage making its way through the mass of people could be heard over the momentary silence which had fallen on the belligerents, the flat accents of the members rose as they urged the men to move aside.

Then arose from the gutter Mr. Dinny Heggarty, bleeding, half sobered, and rushed upon Kane-Norton, bellowing 'God save Ireland!' as he came. He was a huge man; there was no time for a blow, and for a minute it seemed as if Kane-Norton must be smothered in the embrace. The men reeled and spun upon the pavement, while the crowd held its breath, too interested to help in any way. Clean tweeds and dirty frieze wheeled and twisted, with the Boy and Travers spinning with them lest some unfair fist should descend upon their friend. Then the Englishman disengaged himself and backed away. Heggarty looked down on him.

'Ye gave me no room before, but I'll end yer days for ye now,' he roared, and bore down on Kane-Norton, his eyes ablaze, foam on his beard, his face like an angry bull's.

His huge hands shot out, with swinging blows which would have felled an ox, but Kane-Norton dodged cleverly: then came the clean smack of the blow,

and Dinny dropped once more, a huge mass of writhing, furious humanity, howling with mingled pain and anger.

The crowd hummed like an angry beehive, and the Boy found himself wondering how many of these excited people it would take to rush him down; also he felt an anticipatory tingle of a muddy boot hitting his head when he was down.

Dinny Heggarty raised a confused form from the pavement. 'Begorra! that was a fearsome blow,' he said ruefully; he was too giddy at the moment to wish to renew the fight. At this moment the carriage reached them, the sober old horses thrusting the excited human beings aside, and its occupants came to the rescue. Moreover, there was a whisper that the police were somewhere on the outskirts of the row. The two men in the landau listened to the explanations proffered by everyone at once.

'He wouldn't say "God save Ireland!" but he struck Dinny the finest blow ye iver saw in yer life!' yelled a voice.

'Me God, sirs I do ye know that ye might very easily have been killed?' said the smaller of the two men in a tone of fright. He was O'Hara, the member for Cahirvally. As a paid patriot he was completely objectionable; as a man he was a good-natured little fellow with a ready tongue, and this was the side visible now. Magee, the other man, also looked frightened.

'Be the holy Powers! the little man carries a lump of lead within his fists/ remarked Dinny from his lowly position, dipping a huge muddy pocket-handkerchiei in the gutter, and gently rubbing his cheek.

The crowd swayed to the words as easily as they had swayed to anger a little while before.

'Isn't he a great little felly, an' Dinny two heads over him!'

Kane-Norton was five feet ten, but Dinny was a mighty giant of six feet four.

'They so few an' we so many!' chimed in another voice. 'Listen to O'Hara, the mimber, now askin' thim into the cyar. Faix, he'd have been angered av we'd broke their heads for

thim. Afther all, he's English; why wouldn't he be savin' his King?'

Dinny Heggarty proved that he was of a generous disposition; he gave his forehead another dab, and held up a huge hand.

'The divil a sowl iver knocked Dinny before,' he said good-humouredly—' sorra a wan. There's magic in yer fists. An' I wouldn't bear ill-will to the only man that's able. We fought it out man to man.'

Kane-Norton thought of that Dervish dance on the pavement, and shuddered.

Dinny struggled to his feet, his head towering above the crowd as the church-spire towered above the houses all round.

The sparkle was dying out of Kane-Norton's eyes, his habitual languor was assuming sway; but he was quick to recognise generosity, and held out his hand willingly, then turned, anxious to get away.

But Dinny, having a few minutes ago incited the populace to kill him, now felt he must make amends, and he knew but one way. Also he was partially sobered, and he yearned to be drunk again.

'Come an' have a dhrink, sir,' he said, 'to show there's no ill friendship betune us. Faix, dhrink the King's health av ye choose. Maybe, if he heard ov it, he might give us Home Rule, as well as pass us a Land Act'— this with a twinkle in his open eye.

The crowd were overquick to catch the word.

'A dhrink! a dhrink! Surely, now! To make friends. Below at Patsey Toomey's.'

Kane-Norton, horrified, strove to back away, but Travers stopped him. The M.P. whispered, too, at the other side:

'Ye'd better, reely. Please do; they'll be most offinded if ye don't—mortally offinded, indeed.'

Dinny, beaming affability out of the one gray eye, swayed towards Kane-Norton.

'Name what ye like, yer honour, but don't refuse to have a dhrink wid me. An' if ye'll tell me yer name'

Kane-Norton tendered it unwillingly.

Dinny received it with a beam; his great self did nothing by halves.

'Here, boys, let a cheer for Misther KaneNorthon, the only man that was iver able to knock Dinny Heggarty; an' in me time I've played handicuffs wid many a man bigger than yerself.'

He stooped politely to pick up the remains of Kane-Norton's hat; it was chiefly represented by a muddy brim. This, with the best intentions in the world, he crammed down on to its unfortunate owner's head, so that the mud ran down over Kane-Norton's face. Then he took the shrinking Englishman by the arm, and urged O'Hara, as a special honour, to join the party.

So, with Dinny Heggarty at one side and the Nationalist member for Cahirvally at the other, Kane-Norton, the elegant, was swept towards Patsey Toomey's public-house, Travers and the Boy, engulfed by a wave of those who thought they had borne sufficient part in th; fray to join in, following them. The crowd, or, rather, its fringe, opened to let them through, then surged cheerily in their wake.

'Three cheers now for Misther KaneNorthon!' said Dinny.

With the horror of his shouted name tingling in his ears, they wheeled into the street they had come from, Kane-Norton's muddy circlet embracing his triumphant brow, his collar open, his tie flying out, his cheek bleeding from the blow of a stick. Dinny lurched beside him, streaked with much dirt, one eye closed, and the great bump standing out on his cheek, and at the other arm the neat little member, trotting to keep pace with the big men's long strides, and pouring advice into the Englishman's ear as he went.

'Ye don't know what an Irish crowd are, or ye'd niver have been so venturesome. They're like one man, and they'd kill anyone when their blood's up. Ye ran great risk, Mr. Norton—ye did indeed.'

Dinny arrested his progress at a wide dingy door, from which poured a noisome odour of many dead drinks.

'Ye're a man, sir,' said Dinny misti-ly, always with a view to being an orator, as he rubbed the lump on his cheek.

Kane-Norton gasped; he looked at the filthy public-house, at the swaying, drunken crowd. Yet his one idea was to do anything, to drink anything, if it would take him away. Dinny clung to his arm, wheeling him round to face the following multitude, that all might see them and their honourable scars of war. O'Hara, still clinging to the other arm, smiled benevolently. He felt that he had restored good-humour.

'Ye're a man, I tell ye,' repeated Dinny more mistily than before.

Then came a clattering of hoofs, a shouting of voices, a hustle of police; the people opened to let through a carriage, drawn by prancing, frightened horses, a policeman at their heads. Kane-Norton looked at it. Then his senses whirled; he clutched his hatbrim, he strove to back away, but Dinny held him in a grip of iron. For in that carriage was Lady Cahir, clad in velvet and sables, a toque of violets drawn across her powdered face. She was taking her fourth drive through the town of Cahirvally, and her horrified eyes gazed straight into those of Kane-Norton. She was accompanied by her daughters, Doreen and Norah. Their faces were convulsed by repressed laughter, their mother's set in stony horror. And Kane-Norton read a recognition in the look. He was to have lunched there in a few days.

Heggarty merely saw a carriage cleaving its way through the crowd. If, in his muddled state, he thought about it at all, he probably imagined it was the member's landau.

'Ye shall niver say,' he roared, his mighty voice rising above the hum of the crowd, 'that, if we did have words, I did'n' thrate ye dacent afterwards. Dinny's the by who respects a man that can use his fists. Come, yer honour, Misther Kane-Northon. Come, Misther O'Hara.'

'Drive on,' came in faint, icy tones from the carriage. 'Let us get away from this.'

Dinny whirled the two round into the open, odorous door just as the carriage drew level.

'Give it a name, sir,' he said proudly, producing a greasy leather purse.

'Brandy — neat,' muttered Kane-Norton weakly, feeling that temporary oblivion would be a merciful matter.

His acquaintance with Lady Cahir never progressed very much further.

CHAPTER VII HOW THE BOY BECAME A POACHER

There was no doubt about it: the Boy had a taste for low company. Out hunting he spent much of his time joking with the Caseys or their compeers, and on off-days he took his bicycle—it was a much-enduring machine, and had to take the rough with the smooth—and penetrated into the country by himself. Travers and Kane-Norton went to shoot with the local magnates; the Boy preferred to take his gun and search the wild bogs and hillsides. It was his nature to make friends; ere long he had made the acquaintance of a disreputable poacher, a squat, bandy-legged ruffian who went by the name of Mickey the Tramper. This worthy knew every corner of the county, every inch of squelchy bog and gorsy slope. One might almost have thought that the fairies came in the night to tell him where the brown snipe rested on their long, thin legs, where a stray cock was hiding in the hedges, or the flocks of plover rested. The Boy encountered Mickey one day when he had penetrated a tempting-looking bog, unaware of its ownership. Mickey was there, too, full of greater knowledge, but not the least disturbed by the fact that the land was the Doyles' and strictly preserved. From that hour arose a friendship which proved to be lasting.

The poacher was always accompanied by a dog of equally disreputable appearance, a cross between a red setter and a water-spaniel, a most marvellously intelligent brute. From the advent of Mickey the expeditions became more frequent. The bicycle was left at some house, and Mickey and he would strike off across the fields, gray Irish skies overhead, soft winds in their faces, walking over the flat bogs where the deep-brown-hued pools glimmered against the browner background, sometimes leaping from tussock to tussock with slimy death lurking beneath their quick feet, crawling along quietly, the disreputable dog ranging. Then a sudden stiffening of its woolly body, a tiny brown thing against the sky-line, the quick report of a gun rolling across the stillness, sometimes a second, and then the hoarse 'paff'' of Mickey's old single-barrelled muzzle-loader, a rush on the part of Biddy, the queer brown dog, or an expression of absolute disgust waving over her sharp face; she had no patience with bad shots. Anon they were crawling on their stomachs up a long hedgerow, thorns thick above them, friendly brambles hooking them anywhere they could find hold, breathless, mute, muddy—all to get a shot at a cock which, Mickey was informed on the best authority, was lying above in the brake, 'the schamer.'

The bag was trifling, but the Boy loved it all. He grew to know everyone, to hail the farmers as old friends, and to talk their idioms with the brogue of the stage Irishman.

One of Mickey's peculiarities was that he never missed his bird. 'Begorra, now, the feather carried it away!' he would mutter disconsolately, or, 'Did ye see him, yer honour, an' the two legs hangin', an' he off?' Biddy refused to attend to these explanations; her tail would droop miserably, an expression of sour disbelief mantle her brown face.

Mickey possessed no game license; it is doubtful if he would have cared to deal death under its protection, just as Biddy would probably have sickened and died if the Crown had benefited by her life to the extent of half a crown. Force of habit always made Mickey exclaim to the Boy to 'sthick the bird within the hedge,' if a member of the police hove in sight—that is, if it was a stranger; for Mickey said, 'there were many dacent felleys in the force.'

Kane-Norton would have gone home at the first hint of this sort; the Boy grinned with understanding. He never inquired too closely whose land they were shooting over, and made no objection to retreating with undignified haste

when, on rare occasions, some figure appeared on the sky-line which Mickey objected to, and with a hasty glance at it would remark that, 'faix, they'd thry another sphot as quick as they could.' That was Mickey's polite way of putting it.

Once the haste became a sprint, for the man was fairly near before they saw him, and Mickey whispered that it was a personal ' inimy' of his, whom he wouldn't meet for the world. It must be said that the 'inimy' showed a lively desire to hold speech, pursuing at the double, with many distant exhortations, perhaps proffers of new friendship, borne faintly on the breeze. The Boy was fleet of foot; he enjoyed it immensely, and they did not go there again for some time.

It was during one of these expeditions that the Boy struck on a vein of Irish romance and became a match-maker.

There was one gorse-grown hill, with a stream gurgling deep in a narrow ravine, which was one of their most favoured hunting-grounds. That they had leave to shoot there was, in Mickey's eyes, its one drawback. The ground by the gorses was full of rabbit-holes. Halfway down the hill the stream broadened out to an emerald-hued quagmire, where, 'if there was a shnipe above ground,' he might be found. With a touch of frost crisping the earth it was almost a certainty. The stream ran on downwards, losing itself in a boggy trench which bordered wretched rush-grown pastures. The hillside was fair to look at when the sun touched the big gorse-bushes, but it was not land to make money off. Scorched in summer, bare in winter, a few sheep picked up a scanty living there. The hay off the low-lying meadows was half full of rushes; the potatoes grown in the patch of tillage generally got the blight.

Martin Tracy, the man who rented the land, took it all as a matter of course. He lived in the thatched house halfway down the hill, a tumbledown cabin with a manure-heap before the crazy door, a heap of turf helping to keep up the walls at the back, and a general look of poverty about it all. Needless to say, Martin had very little to do; he was an

old friend of Mickey the poacher, and would come tearing to meet them, full of some ' burrd' which he had seen above in the hedge, or to aid them in creeping upon the thoughtless bunnies.

Now, to crawl at close quarters under gorsebushes, with the world blotted into a haze of green, promotes acquaintance; to partake afterwards, when you are violently hungry, of steaming half-baked soda loaf, fresh from an oven, hidden in glowing turf, and swimming in salt butter, washed down by strong tea or buttermilk, promotes love.

Mickey, who was of a restless disposition, would go off to 'hear tell' of further quarry, leaving the Boy munching at this novel fare, given with the true enjoyment which an Irishman takes in seeing anyone devour his substance. The Boy sat in the nook in the wide sooty chimney, generally with the wheel of the bellows in his hand. He took a childish delight in watching the turf redden and glow, and, as the wind came from under the stone flag, seeing the shower of golden sparks fly up into the blackness.

Martin was a big, good-humoured man; he had a merry face and twinkling blue eyes. But at times he was given to sighing, and his eyes grew sad, and one day when the dusk was falling, and the Boy sat with his shooting-boots steaming in the red turf ashes, he asked Martin what the trouble was. The Boy was one of those impecunious people who think a little money never matters; he scented some shortness of rent, and thought he might be able to help. Then it all tumbled out.

The farm, surely, was bad, and scarcely paid, but they talked of draining it some day for him, and then 'twould be good. But as it was, he was poor, no match, 'an' there was a shlip of a girl down beyant there—they were courtin' on the sly this year back—an' now there was a match being made, an' she was to be given to ould Andy Magrath above at Kilcaskin, who had buried two wives already, an' was only afther the girl becaise she had a cow for a fortin'—the divil slheep wid the ould aunt who had died and left the bashte to her!' The blue eyes were suspiciously dark as Martin spoke; it was plain that he was honestly in love. 'I couldn't do much for her,' he said, waving his hand round the bare cabin. 'But, at laste, we'd niver want, an' I'm thinkin' she wouldn't mind much. If the rint went down a taste, an' they dhrained thim fields for me, she might dhrive to Mass wid the besht of thim some day.'

'Andy Magrath? That's the old fellow with a small bog just below his land? I've been there.'

The Boy smoked thoughtfully, considering the question. Could nothing be done? He suggested what would have been his own method of procedure— running away with the girl—but Martin looked so horrified that he gave that up.

As he walked to the road with Mickey that evening, he extracted much information concerning Andy, and ere long was master of that worthy's complete history. From the first wife he had married, to the last, which he was trying to marry, Mickey knew everything. Andy, it appeared, was still bargaining, and had hovered for some time between pretty Norah Magee and a certain Mary Kennedy.

'But, faith, Norah s a darlin' fine girl,' remarked Mickey, 'an', as their fortins are about aquel, he's goin' for the best of thim; only I hears tell that he wants a few geese along wid the cow, an' Norah's father isn't too willing to give thim, so 'tisn't all settled yit.'

This brought them to the highroad, and the Boy got on his bicycle; but he pondered so much over it all on his way back that he descended twice—with rapidity—from the footpath, on which, with true Irish lawlessness, he rode, and scraped his leg severely on a pig's feeding-trough which reposed at a cabin door. The old woman and the pig, who were disputing over the food in some way, clearly thought that he was a bolt from heaven as he descended on them without warning, and fled, shrieking, the pig waking the echoes, the old lady calling on all the feminine gods she could think of. This scrape helped to keep the matter fresh in his mind, and his silence during the evening quite distressed Hannah Anne, who adored him.

A day or two after that the Boy went out shooting by himself. The miles went whirring backwards under his wheels until he jumped off and rolled his bicycle up a stony lane which led to Andy Magrath's house. The moist dimness of Martin's blue eyes haunted him, and he was searching for a plan. Andy was at home, standing at his door. He was a sly-looking old fellow with a bristling white beard and a nutcracker nose and chin. His age was well past sixty; altogether, he did not look like a bridegroom. The Boy hailed him cheerily. Fortunately, they had made friends before, and once the Boy had left the old fellow a hare, which delighted him greatly. It made a dinner.

'Is that you, Misther Rivers? Ye're welcome, sir.' The sun shone, but the ground was in the cold grip of a light frost. 'Go down an' look for a bird, and thin come back an' have a dhrop to dhrink.'

The Boy laid his gun against the railings.

'In a minute,' he said, beginning to light his pipe. He looked round the farm. Good sound pasture, well fenced, wide fields of tillage; a hay-barn, with its stout sides oozing, stood behind the house. The place looked prosperous.

'I hear you're to be married shortly,' said the Boy carelessly. 'By Jove I you ought to be a rich man, all the rich wives you've had.'

Andy considered. 'Faith, I don't know,' he said dispassionately; 'between the bringin' 'em in an' the puttin' 'em out there isn't much to be made on thim.'

The Boy found something very absorbing in his gun; his shoulders shook. Old Andy gazed out over the fields.

'And the next one?' asked the Boy— ' Will she have a great fortune?'

'Great, is it?' Andy spat contemptuously. 'Wan cow! Hadn't Maggie Doolan, that the fever took—God rest her sowl!—a fine twoyear-ould colt, a calf, tin geese, six pounds in banknotes, and the finest feather-bed? An' hadn't Mary Cassidy, who wint wid a cowld — God rest her sowl!—wan hunthred pounds in goold, an' two pigs ready for the market?' The old man's face began to work avariciously. 'And this wan—she has but the cow. But both me sons is dead, an' I'm looking for some wan to come afther me here, so I put me eye on the fine strong girls. Maggie Doolan, now, was always a whisht crature, an' Mary, she had a lame sthep. I can go widout the big money now. The daughters widin are a great help. 'Twill be well indade for Thady Magee's daughter to be sittin' inside there, with help for the work, an' to lie above on Maggie's bed.'

The Boy looked round at the farm, then back at the house, where one of the ugly daughters was feeding the fowls, and lastly at Andy himself, with his lean, ill-looking face, and he shook his head, thinking that even the privilege of lying on the dead Maggie's featherbed might be too dearly purchased.

'I suppose all women are much the same/ said the Boy, with what he hoped might be fine diplomacy. 'And, then, you'll have to give fortunes to your girls. With all this you might get a richer wife.'

There was something in the Boy's voice which invited confidence. Andy nodded his bald head. 'Thrue for ye,' he said; 'but I've money now, and I can look for a young wan. There's Mary Moylan, now, another fine lump of a girl, but there was no differ in thare fortins, and Norah is a purty darlin'.'

His old eyes took an expression which made the Boy want to shake the owner.

'Well'—Andy waved his pipe—' the match is near made. If ye'll come to the weddin', sir, we'll make ye very welcome. I'll stroll down wid ye now, an" we'll see if we can find a bird in the bog.'

A little later, declining Andy's offer of a drink, the Boy made his way across to Martin's farm, and for the first time saw the Norah Magee in question. To be accurate, she was in Martin's arms as he came up. They disengaged themselves slowly, merely looking slightly sheepish; it was the Boy who blushed. Norah was a pretty, dark girl, with eyes which matched her lover's. She was very young, not more than eighteen, so had had no time to grow careworn. The Boy began to understand the look in Martin's face. He had never been in love himself, but he could sympathize.

He sat down on a damp bank and talked to them seriously. He counselled them to run away and have done with it. Pretty Norah and old Andy could never be endured. This pair of fine young animals were made for each other. He mapped it all out—how he himself would drive them to Traheen, how they could be married there before the registrar—he felt sure there would be a registrar—come back, and then the priest would marry them afterwards. They refused to listen to him. To be wed without 'bell, book, and candle' was clearly something on an equality with going to Purgatory straight away. They would have none of him. Norah wept, and invoked the saints to witness that it was a black day on which she first saw the light Martin rumbled curses, muttering that 'he wished the divil had ould Andy be the throat, and was to git three sowls if he squz the life out of him." There was nothing further to be said. From Norah's tearful utterances, it appeared that the match was very nearly made; the wedding would be before Shrove, and nothing short of a miracle could rescue her.

The Boy left-them after a little, and strolled on, in a bad temper with the world. He went on aimlessly until he reached a wood, into which he went to sit down and think. It was no joke to try to help the Irish. Gleams of sunlight touched the log he sat on; the ground beneath his feet was covered with thick green moss, and the pungent scent of fir-trees and fallen cones reached his nostrils. The Boy sat with his head down, something stirring in his blood. So far life had contented him; now he felt lonely.

'Do you know you're trespassing?' said a voice close to him.

He started up, to see Miss Maguire standing close to him. She wore her usual hard sailor hat and short tweed dress, but her clear skin glowed in the crisp air; the sun picked out golden threads in her fair hair.

'Sorry,' he said. 'But can one trespass in Ireland?'

She raised her hand, pointing out a warning board which was fixed just above his head.

'It's just as well my keepers didn't catch you with your gun and something in your gamebag,' she said severely.

'I could have settled them,' he said, with the confidence born of many dealings with keepers.

'Not mine,' she answered firmly.

But the Boy's thoughts were far from keepers.

They were filled with Norah and Martin and old Andy Magrath.

'I'm involved in a love trouble,' he said. 'My head's full of it, and I came in here to sit and think.'

'Oh,' said Miss Maguire stiffly — 'Miss Clancy?'

'It's not my own,' said the Boy hastily. 'I never was in love. I only care for sport. It's some people here.'

'Tell me,' said Sheila Maguire, the stiffness dying out of her voice.

'Oh—I—but you'd be sure to let it out,' said the Boy dubiously.

'Thank you,' said the lad)'. 'You are always polite.'

'I don't mean anything,' he assured her hastily, for either the sunlight flickered on her face or it worked a little. 'I only mean no woman can keep secrets, and you know all these people here—and'

She began to move away; then she turned and looked at him as he leant against his tree. 'You're always down on me,' she said quietly.

'And you certainly are on me,' retorted the Boy with hasty truth. 'But look here'—he yearned to unburden himself; his heart felt strangely heavy, strangely lonely—' will you listen?' He began to pour out his story. 'And I'd give anything to help them. But what can I do?' he concluded at last.

Miss Maguire leant against another tree, and listened with interest. 'I can understand your being sorry,' she said. 'But you know they buy and sell each other as if they were cows at a fair.

It's foolish to help. If Norah married Martin, she would probably regret the featherbed and the side-car in a year or two. H'm I Andy—Mary Moylan I Do you know, I think it's a good thing you told me. The Moylans are tenants of mine.'

'What have you thought of?' he inquired eagerly.

'I'll tell you later,' she said, smiling. 'Now good-bye; and—let me warn you: if the keepers —especially the Scotch one—catch you here uninvited, they'll be nasty to you.'

Under these circumstances, the Boy forbore to speak of the shoot which he and Mickey had had in this wood a short time before. He had not known it was preserved. Mickey avoided noticeboards.

'We—they fancy they heard shots here some days ago,' she continued, with a shade of suspicion in her voice.

The Boy remarked that he had always heard that Ireland was full of poachers.

'There's one called Mickey,' said Miss Maguire.

'I have seen him," said the Boy truthfully, with the expression of a cherub, and wondering how much the lady knew.

'We shoot on Thursday; will you come out with the other two?' she asked abruptly, the invitation clearly costing her an effort, for she stirred the grass with her foot.

'Oh, two of us are enough,' the Boy hastened to assure her. 'I am going to wander over the bogs with—with a man. He has invited all the "burrds" in the country to be ready for me.'

'Oh, if you prefer that!' she said, going off. Then, turning: 'I'll not forget your love-birds.' Though her big white house stood in sight, she did not ask the Boy in, and at that moment he would have been glad of some tea.

'Seems a pity,' said the Boy to himself, 'that the heiress should have such a fixed dislike to me. I might have come to stop there when one or other of those fellows catches her. For I shall never desert Cahirvally if I can help it. But she wouldn't have me to stay.'

He strode away for his bicycle, and

was suddenly confronted by Martin and his girl in a wild state of excitement. 'We'll do itr yer honour,' cried Martin; 'Norah says she will if ye'll help us. We'll cheat ould Andy, after all.'

The Boy was honestly pleased. He sat down—fortunately, damp had no effect on his constitution—and talked rapidly. It seemed a pity that the only time Norah dared run away should be about eleven at night, when everyone was asleep, as the Boy could not quite reason out what they were to do at Traheen until it became light. But when you start abducting people you must take the rough with the smooth; and he let the hour stand. The two hung on his words breathlessly. The flight was for Wednesday night.

'On this side of the wood, then, at half-past ten on Wednesday,' were the Boy's last words.

'Well, what of your love-birds?' Miss Maguire asked him next day; but in his state of high tension he thought that heartless, and merely shook his head.

He determined that he would not tell the others where he was going to. So on Wednesday night he hired Maddigan with injunctions to be prepared for a long journey, and, armed with his gun to give colour to the duck-shooting expedition which he said he was bent on, he sallied forth.

All day the country had lain under a murky fog, with battalions of copper-edged clouds on the horizon. It was a dark, still night, starless, with a faint sough of rising wind as the hour grew later. The hedges loomed, black wraiths out of the gloom. Now and again the moon, though hidden, brightened the sky, and they could see the clouds racing in the currents above. Every cabin was shut up; there was not a light anywhere. The Boy shivered sleepily, wishing himself at home. Maddigan, wondering what mad prank was on foot, drove on steadily, the gray mare's shoulders butting the darkness. They reached the fir-wood, towering black against the dimness.

'Wait here,' said the Boy, as he jumped down. He absently took his gun with him. There was no sound of any-

one, and, thinking the two were hiding inside, he climbed the bank bordering the road. The darkness was inky in the shelter of the trees. He peered round, listening, but the place was full only of the noises of a wood at night—whispers among the trees, branch creaking to branch, sleepy twitters from the roosting birds. The Boy banged up against a stump, and swore softly. There was only one explanation: they must have mistaken the side. The wood ran between two roads; he remembered that. He began to make his way across; the wood grew thicker as he advanced. It was full of undergrowth, and the brambles seemed like live snakes reaching out to catch him. A gleam of light told he had reached the other side. After the gloom of the wood he could see almost clearly, but there was no sign of anyone. He leant against the fence, peering down the road. He struck a match, looking at his watch; they were already half an hour behind time, and if they were not with Maddigan by now, something must have happened.

But sounds at last — footstep coming stealthily.

'Come on, now,' he said cautiously; 'you're very late.'

'Get round them,' said a strong Scotch accent. 'Now the lantern—turn it on. We have the rascils, certain.'

He smelt the odour of hot metal, he heard the whispers, and—the truth burst on him. These footsteps were not for him. They heralded the approach of Miss Maguire's keepers, looking for poachers. There was still time to stroll out, explaining casually; but he felt the gun in his hands, he thought of the sorry explanation he could make, and, as a shaft of light cut suddenly across the blackness, he took cover. The wood was wide; if he could once reach Maddigan, all might yet be well. He wriggled through the undergrowth, and the footsteps came nearer.

'I heard him speak,' said a stealthy voice. 'Call the dog here, Dick.'

The dog—he heard it sniff—meant discovery. The Boy rolled silently towards the hedge; this was a matter for his heels. He clung to the wet bank,

squirmed up it, rolled down into a foot of water in the ditch beyond, and reached the road outside. He slipped across this in the shadows, and all might have gone well with him, but, as he tried to get over the other fence, some treacherous stones rattled under his feet, and in a passing gleam of moonlight they saw him.

A view-halloo rang out, the undergrowth crackled as the keepers burst through it, the dog yelped at his heels.

The Boy was a fast runner, but it was a strange country and very dark; he had nothing to guide him. The dog speedily overtook him, but he confused its intelligence by cheering it on in search of some further foe, and, greatly puzzled, it ceased yelping and ran beside him.

He tumbled into black, thorny pitfalls; he splashed into ditches; he tumbled over banks. The soft night air rushed past him in the dimness, and the Boy wondered when the dark world would come to an end, and when his breath would finally give out. Then a high, dark mass loomed up before him, and he saw that it was a wall. Hope seemed over, but, fortunately, it was an Irish wall; there were loose places in the masonry, and the Boy swarmed up it, gun and all, the dog wailing mournfully beneath it.

'He's over here," trumpeted the panting Scotch voice. 'We must mak' the gate, James.'

'Mak' the divil!' groaned the Boy, as he bolted into the shrubbery without the faintest idea of where he was going, until suddenly he ran out among some trim flower-beds, and saw that he had run to Miss Maguire's square white house, black now in the shadows, but with one patch of light illuminating its gloom. He made for that, and as his hurried footsteps sounded on the gravel a terrier darted out at him, and Miss Maguire's figure appeared, outlined clearly by the lamp behind her.

'Have you caught them?' she asked.

'No, but they're catching me,' said the Boy desperately.

Miss Maguire was sitting up to see her Scotch keeper as he went homewards. They had been a good deal troubled by poachers of late, and were making strenuous efforts to catch them. She went to speak to the keeper, and was confronted by the vision of the Boy, hatless, breathless, his clothes torn, his face scratched, his gun trailing behind him.

'For God's sake, as I've run so far, hide me,' said the Boy, 'so that the Scotchman won't catch me. I always hated the nation. Oh! I'll never go match-making again.'

'Match-making? Poaching,' said Miss Maguire severely.

'Match-making,' repeated the Boy. 'I was abducting Martin and Norah on a car to

Traheen. We were to have met by that d

—I beg your pardon, wood. They never turned up, but your keepers did, and went for me when I took them for the lovers. Then I lost my head, and ran, and—here I am.'

Miss Maguire took a chair weakly; she shook from smothered laughter, but she invited the Boy to come in.

Then, as she laughed, the sound of heavy footsteps sounded outside.

'Hide me,' said the Boy.

'I must now, for my own sake,' she said. 'Sandy would give warning if he knew I had harboured a poacher.'

She pushed him behind the curtain, and went to the window. 'Thank heaven!' she said, ' Mrs. Moore has gone to bed.'

She called to the men as they came up panting, and the Boy heard with much relish the Scotchman's breathless account of how they had lighted on a poacher—' wid the legs of a hare,' the under-keeper put in ruefully;—how they had tracked him across country until they had found the dog—on which he had cast some spell—barking under the wall; how the villain had a car waiting to carry off his spoils, which car had fled at their first approach.

The Boy blessed Maddigan.

All this and much more the Scotchman poured out, until finally Miss Maguire suggested that he was losing all chance of catching his man, and directed him to a distant part of the grounds, where she had heard the footsteps running to. The keepers vanished, calling off their dog, which had discovered the Boy behind his curtain, and was sniffing at his friend or enemy, he scarcely knew which.

Then the Boy came, shamefacedly for him, into the room. The situation did not lack embarrassment.

It was a pretty, old-fashioned little room, with roomy, chintz-covered chairs, and a collection of good sporting prints hung on the wall. The tall girl looked at him, her light blouse showing her fair skin to its best advantage. Her hair was looser than usual; she looked more womanly and less selfreliant.

'Well?' she said. 'Are you always in scrapes?'

'Seems so,' said the Boy ruefully.

'You want something to drink badly,' she said; 'but I can't call the servants to get it for you. The only thing I can do is to lend you a cap and show you the road home.'

The Boy was still silent. Then, as Sheila Maguire put on a hat, he broke into speech.

'Where could they have gone to?' he said.

'Martin is probably sleeping soundly,' said Miss Maguire, 'and Norah is telling her beads, and praying to the Virgin to forgive her for having thought of running away.'

'But they looked so awfully in love,' said the Boy; 'so unhappy, too, and I thought'

'You meant well,' she said, as they went out into the soft night. 'But love is a transient passion with those people.' Her lips tightened.

The night had cleared; a small moon rode in the sky. They paused at the wicket-gate leading out on to the road, and she held out her hand to him.

'Will you come to shoot in the morning, after all?' she asked.

'I never want to see that wood again,' said the Boy, from the depths of his heart; then, conscious that this was slightly ungracious, he added: 'Of course, if you wish me to come—if you want a gun, I'll be delighted.'

'Oh, don't put yourself out,' she an-swered coldly, and the shake of the laughter seemed still to cling to her voice. Her face was in shadow. 'I assure you, I do not want a gun.'

The Boy uttered some awkward thanks, and they parted. He looked back when he had walked some little way, and saw her tall figure still standing in the gateway, outlined by the moon behind it, framed by the black of the woodwork. Then he remembered that many girls would have been afraid to come out alone in the night, and that she had taken a great deal of trouble for him.

Far down the road to Cahirvally the Boy found Maddigan. There was no sign of the lovers. He flung his chagrined, weary self on to the car, and bade Maddigan drive to the devil as fast as he conveniently could. Maddigan remarked that he thought they had a long journey to go, and without any questioning turned for home. As the mare's hoofs rang out and the miles slipped away, the Boy's tongue loosened, and he spoke of his misfortunes. He still concealed the reason of his starting on this midnight expedition, however, and it is doubtful if the carman thought him entirely innocent.

In the early morning, long ere the Boy was up, Hannah Anne announced that a ' felly was below who said he must see his honour imtnadiate. There was a matther of a murdher in it,' she thought, 'judging from the things he was bawlin' below,' and in the depths of his bed the Boy learnt from Martin, who was incoherent from sorrow, what had happened.

Norah had been caught 'be an old a'nt— may the divil himself see to her roastin'!'—and brought back. He, waiting outside, had heard the racket. Of course she had denied all guiltiness, and never said where she was going; but, at all events, it had rendered the flight hopeless for that night, and this morning, 'stealin' out to him' in the gray dawning, she had declared that the ' hand of Hivin was agin her, and she would let things be.'

The Boy despatched the sorrowing Martin, and gave the whole thing up as a bad job. In his rambles he kept away from the part of the country which reminded him of his failure. He did not care to speak of it to anyone, for he was very sorry for Martin and the girl. Miss Maguire, too, seemed to fight shy of the subject and his midnight raid; she was colder than ever to him when they met, and he kept well away from her out hunting, so that they never even spoke of the affair, nor did she tell anyone else.

A month later he found himself, his gun in his hand, near Andy's house. He had not meant to come, but the bog was tempting. It was a soft February day, gray clouds fleeting overhead, a caress of warmth in the west wind. Mickey, the faithful, tramped beside him. Mickey had not been allowed to gossip lately, and the Boy knew nothing of Andy's doings. The old man was probably married, for it was an early Lent. He looked round, dreading to see Norah's pretty face, bathed in gloom. Andy was standing at his door in his old attitude, beside him a big, ill-favoured woman, a bucket of pig's food in her hand.

'Begor, ye've deserted us lately,' Andy greeted him warmly. 'An' we lookin' for ye to ask ye to the weddin', sir.'

Again the Boy looked for Norah. 'Where's your wife?' he asked.

'This is Mrs. Magrath, sir.'

'This! This!' The Boy stared at the big, ugly woman. 'But I thought—I thought'

'Oh, surely, Norah—well, the match was almost med betune us; but Mary Moylan here, she was always great wid Miss Maguire above, an' the lady guv her a fine cow to have as a fortin whin she married, an' she had wan before. So Mary havin' two cows, an' Norah Magee but wan, I changed me mind, for sure yer honour knows that there isn't the differ of a cow betune any two women in the world.'

Mary, the bride, smiled affably at this. The Boy checked a rising inclination to cheer.

'And—Norah?' he inquired, trying to make his voice a careless one.

'Norah, is it? Well, then, as she missed such a big match'—here Mary smirked once more—' they're marryin' her to that poor fellow Martin Tracy, in consideration, I hear, that his land is goin' to be dhrained shortly. Faith, I think they went to chapel yesterday. Poor girl! 'twas a chance I got through her father houldin' out about thim geese I wanted wid the cow.'

The Boy refused a pressing invitation to go and drink. He left some happy 'burrd' to live in the bog, and made at his best pace for Martin's cabin. Perhaps he, too—Andy was doubtful—was already married.

'Bravo, Miss Maguire!' he shouted, as he got out of sight of Andy's house. 'Bravo! You didn't forget them, after all. And I had given up. Bravo again!',.

Mickey, toiling in the rear, smiled affably, wondering if the Boy was slightly drunk.

At the double the Boy topped the hill above Martin's house. The thin spiral of smoke from the chimney hung in the soft air; two figures stood at the door; a red cow grazed in the field.

'I declare she's a *ripper f* said the Boy, as he swung down the descent.

But never as long as he lives will he meddle in the love affairs of the Irish peasantry again.

CHAPTER VIII OF A DINNER-PARTY AND A COWSHED

The eldest Miss Clancy was slightly in love with Norman Rivers, otherwise the Boy. There was a disparity of years between them, the advantage—if you can call extra years an advantage—resting with the lady; but that mattered little.

Madge Clancy had seen a great deal of life. In trying moments in moist flower-gardens, with squelching paths underfoot, and with a draught from heaven to cool sentiment, also in the damp of the mouldy conservatory, where hairy cacti and Wandering Jews disputed supremacy—in these and other places the Boy had held his own.

Tales of the Englishmen's riches had gathered in Cahirvally, gathered until people spoke of them in hushed tones; and the eldest and the other Miss Clancys dreamt dreams of how nice it would be to see the world across St. George's

Channel; to wander, untrammelled by cares, in the vast unknown city, which to them was a mere dream of shops.

Kate Clancy, the youngest, called Baby— a name which always suggests undue age— studied her ladies' papers with extra diligence. The result of these studies was that she announced that it was quite impossible, under the circumstances, to give these aristocratic strangers one of their ordinary dinner-parties— big joints, steaming hot, for papa and mamma to cut, generous helpings of pink-hued beef or white-fleshed turkey, followed by heavy pudding or pie, champagne flowing vigorously throughout. It was all very good to eat; but for years the Miss Clancys had striven to alter it, and introduce the modern things they read of. So far, in vain.

Now, at last, their chance seemed to have arrived. They pleaded with papa, and he was induced to listen. These three Englishmen, coming to their house for the first time, must be impressed and greeted by the latest style. Of course, it was only for this once, the wily girls said; but in their secret hearts they determined that everything should be so perfect that papa should never wish to return to the old ways.

Under the heading of 'Mavourneen' the *Ladies' Guide* answered their questions. Sweets, salted almonds, flowers—nothing else on the table on any account. Everything must be carved behind a screen by the butler. This made the Miss Clancys thoughtful: they had no screen and no butler. But they soon reasoned it out. and set to work.

Travers accepted the invitation with the remark that it would be their first regular dinner-party. They had dined out many times, but this invitation came on a blazoned card and gave them a fortnight's notice.

The Miss Clancys told them coyly, out hunting, that they were 'so glad they could come'; and when the date came round, Maddigan drove them out through a soft night, a south wind moaning across the land, a moon, copperrimmed, seeming to race with the flying scud.

They drove to the shadow of the tall

stone house, an arc of light cutting the blackness before the door.

The Boy took off his coat, sniffing up the wind, remarking that, if it were only daylight, there be 'a tearing scent.' Then they were ushered into the drawing-room, which was lighted with many lights and full of flowers. Its present beauty would really have checked memory if the trail of stale smoke and whisky had not fought with the heavy scent of the narcissi, and beaten down the dainty flowers.

The four Miss Clancys, all in white, swam to meet them, obliterating their mother. Travers thought he shook hands with her; but was not sure. The red heads were auburn at night. The girls were all plump, especially the eldest, and the Boy, gravitating towards her, hoped they would go and see the flowers afterwards. The eldest Miss Clancy was completing his education.

The party numbered twelve, and included two men in short-tailed, tight-trousered evening suits, and a stray girl, introduced as Miss Murphy, who possessed big eyes and a talent for silence. One of the men eyed the Boy moodily as he whispered with Madge Clancy. He was something in an office, and for years had aspired to the hand of the eldest Miss Clancy, vainly, yet there was always an understanding that 'some day,' when she was tired of amusement and he did better, his turn was to come. He had been doing better lately, when the Boy chose to crop up, and the eldest Miss Clancy's heart went once more.

This man, Martin by name, had been specially asked to dinner to-night to endure what his inamorata called 'a trifle of teasing.' The prospect failed to give him appetite.

A shy head poked round the door, a bell clanged wildly outside, and a low voice announced that 'dinner was waitin' on thim.'

Then, as they rose, a furious voice, evidently that of the bell-ringer, rose in high-pitched contempt outside.

'Wisha, thin, Patsey Reidy, after all that I towld ye! Is that the way to be callin' the quality to their meals. One minute I left ye while I shook the bell,

an' ye afeared to put yer nose around the dour!'

Then, after a spirited argument as to their respective ranks, held by the eldest Miss Clancy and her mother, they trooped in to the diningroom.

It was dinner *d la 'rousse':* that is how Kate Clancy rendered it. Under white bodices, cut with due economy about the shoulders, three hearts beat triumphantly. They had arranged, directed, ordered; now would come their reward: papa's heart would melt, and for the future they could entertain in a proper manner. The dining-room at Claheen had, fortunately, lent its aid to their plans. It was next door to the kitchen, and Papa Clancy had connected the two by means of a small square hole in the wall, so that his favourite marrow-bones and toasted cheese might arrive hot. Now all the food was to be carved in the kitchen, as no screen was forthcoming, and was to be handed in through the hole. Two maids assisted, and Patsey, the stable-boy, did duty for the nonexistent butler. A faint and healthy reek of the stables followed him as he clumped about.

Soup was ladled out on the side-table. It was a very thin liquid, and smelt heavily of sherry. Papa Clancy, a big, red-faced man with side-whiskers and an aggressive voice, eyed it suspiciously and partook. His comments were, unfortunately, audible.

'Be jabers, Norah Reidy,' he remarked to the maid, 'They've emptied in the sherry decanter and clean forgotten the soup. Never mind; 'twill do instead of a glass o' wine;' and he supped it up.

Dinner proceeded. Travers took his fish, and, following papa's example with the soup, eyed it suspiciously. It represented those things so dear to the inferior cook—fish balls —and represented them somewhat untidily. It was, however, highly savoury; the onions had not been forgotten.

The youngest Miss Clancy, who sat next to Travers, confided to him, as she took hers, that 'Cahirvally was the hardest place in the world to get a bit of fish in; hadn't Nolan, the fishmonger, been

saving this cod up for days on a taste of ice for them, so as to keep it sweet?'

Travers suddenly felt that his appetite for fish had left him; he began to understand the onions.

Then came entries on heavy silver dishes, with their outsides resplendent, but the insides quite forgotten. Papa stirred the potatoes and paper frills and the compound within dubiously, and Martin became a victim to acute depression. If this was the way in which the eldest Miss Clancy had now elected to live, he felt his chances were few. Clearly, all these things were born of acquaintance with the English. His glance, dark and gloomy, fell once more on the unconscious Boy, who was wondering how much entrde he could conceal, and how much scatter uneaten about his plate. Then came a lull; Patsey vanished from the room, and the reek of horse went with him. Conversation filled up the vacancy, and Kane-Norton, always polite, though his nerves were somewhat tried, thought it was time to break through the wall of reserve which masked the large-eyed maiden on his left. He asked her languidly if she hunted.

She looked at him.

'No,' she answered briefly.

This was pure shyness. Kane-Norton felt condescending and kind. He fixed his eyeglass and pulled his moustache.

'But surely you know all about it in this land of sport?' he said, in tones of condescension which he felt were sure to tell.

They did. The damsel turned her velvety orbs full upon him.

'The divil a haporth,' she said, with her first smile. It was a long speech for her, but she appreciated his civility.

'Eh!' said Kane-Norton weakly, and abandoned the conversation.

The Miss Clancys chattered; the Boy drank champagne and whispered to the eldest Miss Clancy. Martin's brow grew blacker; Papa drummed on the table with a fork, looking at the empty space in front of him. It was evident that a hitch had arisen. Patsey was still absent, and the two maids gathered round the square opening, their voices humming in undertones.

What had happened? Travers stooped to read the little menu-cards, tied up with pink ribbon to match the pink sweets (see *Ladies' Guide),* which were clearly written in her best French, so far as it went, by Madge Clancy.

'Potage de julienne' *'Cotellette de cod'* That had been written before the arrival of the fish; then the cook declared that 'faith, 'twas too far gone for thim stheaks to be med of it, but with a tashte of pepper an' plinty inyins, who'd be the wiser?'

'Olive de bceuf.' They had arrived on the silver dishes with the resplendent outsides.

'Canneton roti, with peas.' *l Bceufroti!*

They had clearly reached this stage, but were only faced by a vacant table and pink sweets.

'Be jabers!' said Papa Clancy and drummed the harder.

The Miss Clancys cast agonized glances kitchenwards; the eldest had nervously begun to push back her chair, when the voices of the maids arose, a sound of heated argument drifted into the room. Somehow, all eyes were drawn to the little square opening. The maids drew back, hopelessly brushed aside by some invisible force, and a red, heated face wa s thrust through the opening. It was the cook's, and her voice rang in anguished tones through the room.

'Oh, if ye plaze, miss, Patsey can make no hand of the docks—no hand at all! And he afraid to tell ye! Fairly mangled he has thim!'...

At this juncture someone pulled her back, the sounds of argument arose once more, and the maids stood aghast.

Kane-Norton's eyeglass went down with a clanging ring against his wineglass, upsetting it; the Boy spluttered audibly, and Miss Murphy added to her conversation for the evening by saying 'Heavenly Powers!' twice over.

Red, shamed red, suffused the cheeks of the four Miss Clancys—red which deepened to crimson when, in obedience to a command from papa, Patsey came in with the ' dooks ' he had wrestled with, and laid their remains on the table.

The beef, fortunately, was whole, if a little chilly.

Baby Clancy was young—she was nigh to tears; indeed, one salty drop did trickle on to her portion of 'dook' when it came to her, carved in stony silence by papa. The family all took duck, because no one else would, and they were afraid the beef might not go round.

Their troubles were not quite over. Peas (bottled) were to have been served with the 'dooks,' but Patsey, who had quite lost his head, brought them in in a covered dish, and laid them at Mrs. Clancy's elbow. He hovered there for a second, oppressed by his moments with the 'dooks,' and wondering what to do next. Biddy and Norah Reidy were flying round the table with laden plates. Patsey grew desperate; anything was better than standing still.

'Will I sthrip the pays, ma'am?' he asked in a hoarse whisper.

Kane-Norton's eyeglass again showed signs of falling.

'What's that, Patsey?' asked Mrs. Clancy, who was a little deaf.

'Will I sthrip the pays, ma'am? Sorra a sowl has a tashte of thim yit.'

He held out a plate which he had captured. He thought that everything ought to go round on plates.

'Patsey!' cried Miss Clancy wildly, as the hoarse tones sounded, 'hand round those vegetables.'

'Oh, glory be to the hivins above!' muttered Patsey, wiping his heated brow. 'But I'd give me place up rather than to be thryin' to plaze the quality agin whin they're atinV

Kane-Norton was by this time past speech; the Boy continued to bury his face in champagne. Martin's brow cleared as Patsey made his way round with the 'pays,' and halted by Miss Clancy's chair, where he was furiously commanded to take the cover off the dish.

'Take it off!' she commanded furiously.

Patsey's temper was wearing thin.

'An', sure, didn't I ask the missus twice if I'd sthrip 'em?' answered the injured boy, as he tucked the cover under his arm.

There were more misfortunes to that ill-fated dinner. The meringues gave way, and had to be helped *en masse.* The savoury looked all right, but it tasted—well, the cook's explanation shows what it was like. Jam and sardine don't mingle. In answer to almost tearful comments next day, she declared that 'she was that floosthered looking at the shape of thim fine dooks that she lost the recaite they give her; but knowin' for certain there was something red below the sardines, she put a fine smauther of jam underneath, and 'twas grand they looked. An' the ladies had no cause to be grumblin; wasn't the look everything an' all?'

But to the guests there were compensations. The champagne was perfection, the port was pallid from age and wisdom, the 'dooks' were forgotten when the time came to eat pink sweets, and four dejected Miss Clancys left the room, to fall in a body upon Patsey in the hall.

Even Kane-Norton, who had suffered a good deal from shock, felt a glow of satisfaction, and thought he would even come again.

'Be jabers '—old Clancy roused himself, and looked with a twinkle in his eye at the square opening, its little door flying wide dejectedly— 'that's the first time that me dinner, barrin' the plates and a marrow bone, was ever handed to me through that place, and, be jabers, 'twill be the last! Norah Reidy, get another bottle of port wine.'

There was no conservatory after dinner, but much may be said behind a big photograph book, and the eldest Miss Clancy, who was on the verge of hysterics, recovered a little as she talked to the Boy.

'Papa had us fairly driven mad,' she confided. 'He *will* slash the meat for everyone—a thing that's never done now—and have even the sweets on the table. At last I had him persuaded to let us do things decently, and now, thanks to that Patsey, 'tis all up. And I showing him half the day yesterday, when the ducks were hanging, how to cut them, and he swearing he could do it as easy as kiss your hands, while the cook was driving away at the beef. We're done for ever, now;' and she was nigh to tears.

The Boy comforted her. He casually introduced some of his relations into the conversation. He assured her that, when his uncle, Lord Bolton, dined with the late Queen—it seemed to have been a matter of everyday occurrence—he had often helped her to carve when she got tired. The old lady quite prided herself on her carving—(Miss Clancy observed, 'Do you say so?' and dried her eyes)—while as for Lord Bolton himself, the Boy went on, *he* prided himself on being the quickest carver in England. They always got him to carve the geese at the Lord Mayor's dinner.

Miss Clancy held up the photograph-book, for when she lowered it she caught the loving glances of Mr. Martin, who sat in happy silence on a sofa with Miss Murphy, his eyes fixed on as much of Madge Clancy as he could see. Sometimes he rose, with the intention of coming over, but invariably sat down again, and resumed the conversation without words.

But the eldest Miss Clancy felt better, and the Boy hoped that these and a few further lies might not be entered against him in the record of his misdeeds, as they were born of kindness and an earnest wish to make the eldest Miss Clancy sleep early and forget the 'docks.'

They drove home from their first Irish dinner-party through the murky softness; the moon had grown tired and was asleep. It was cold; a soft moan of coming rain hung on the wind, and dark clouds raced overhead. Travers says it was sleep which made them all so taciturn on their way home, and so tenacious of their hold on the rails of the car; but the Boy, who was always overtruthful, affirmed it to have been the super-excellence of Mr. Clancy's drink, further helped in its baneful effect by a very light dinner. They roused Hannah Anne from sweet slumber with a feverish inquiry for told meat, and when that damsel, wrapped in a shawl and in her leaden hair-pins, assured them that ' there wasn't a thing cowld in the place but the pig's face she and the missus were afther atin' for their dinner,' they had it up and fell upon it recklessly, helping it down with hunks of warm griddle cakes which, Hannah Anne said, she had 'thrun into the oven to put a taste of heart in thim, the fires bein' banked up agin the morninV

The wind ran round to the south-east in the night, and they awoke to a sound of raging tempest and raw cold. They could see great black clouds humped sulkily on the horizon when they looked out over the cold background of slates from the ' topmosht window.' Snow? It looked like snow, and the meet was many miles away; but hunting is sometimes as much a business as a pleasure, and the three huddled shivering on to the car, driving out into the country with the sting of the wind behind them. The sky was blue still, but the great banks of heavy clouds lurked grimly, and as they drew nearer to the fixture one rose and spread out blackly, cloaking the blue.

The meet was at a gate. Even as they drove up the snow came down, white and blinding, driven by a roaring blast. Snow gathered in humps on pink coats, drove under saddles, soaked down shivering necks. Then the great cloud swept onwards, and the washed blue showed overhead with a gleam of warming sun. The move was made to the covert over a white land, and against a bitter wind.

The gorse lay between two patches of bogland, where the brown pools glimmered darkly amid the surrounding whiteness. Desolate marshy land stretched away to a range of hills, their crests now masked by the murky cloud. The wind howled across the flat land like a live thing.

'And this is pleasure!' said Travers, humping his back with the fallacious idea that it made him warmer, as he sheltered behind a bare thorn-bush.

'Yow!' A note in covert, another, a vista of hounds fleeting swiftly through the gorse, a yell from the whip, and a small brown body creeping away. Hounds poured out in a wave of white and tan, their eager, wistful faces athirst for blood. In a moment they were away—and it was evident that a tearing scent lay on the snowy earth—across the bog, where the rotten banks slid away beneath the horses' feet, skirting peaty holes, plunging through spongy earth, always with a vision of fair green land beyond and the pack running mute on a burning scent.

When he had jumped the last fence out of the bog, Travers sat down to enjoy himself, for Merrylass, like all good hunters, did not want to fall, and topped her banks now. True, she did it with a certain economy—a fleeting tap of one dainty rounded hoof as she went off — but she never fell, and, with ears laid back and disdain in every movement, would even creep down some water-course which in England she would certainly have jumped. But—human hopes are born to die—a plash of something soft yet stinging, a sudden sensation of blackness overhead, and the world was a white one again. Hounds threw up their heads; hunting was impossible. The master turned his back to the wind and sought shelter in some farm buildings. To this day Travers and KaneNorton wish they had stayed oat in the snow.

They all, as many as could find room, crammed into the long cow-house. The snow rushed past outside on the back of the whooping wind. Sir Ralph eyed it disconsolately; it looked like the end of his day's hunting. The horses huddled together. It was cold, even with all the warm life crowded there, their breaths steaming out on the snowy air.

Doyle and Kane-Norton were standing side by side. Their conversation was generally of the frostiest description, but Dick Doyle had got very well away in the morning hunt, and seen Kane-Norton wallowing in a peaty drain. He knew that Miss Maguire had also seen him. It may have been the memory of this which made him forget his animosity and turn to the Englishman with a friendly remark. Then he jerked his hand towards the other side of the yard where a crowd of frieze-coated farmers were standing by a ladder.

'Ever see an Irish inquest?' he asked.

'Can't say that I have.' Kane-Norton

peered across the whirl of snow.

'You've a chance now, then. We're on top of a tragedy here. Michael Reidy's man died suddenly of a bit of a stroke on the head a couple of days ago, and they're seeing him to find out if it was drink or a tap behind. 'Twould be nearly worth your while to hear some of the things that will be said. Call your friends; we'll go across. These men will hold our horses—only don't say what it is, or we'd have the whole hunt on our heels.'

Kane-Norton hesitated, but the cloud looked unbroken, and he was curious—the Irish were such a strange race. He collected Travers and the Boy, and they went across the yard, Donovan Moore, lean and saturnine, watching them with wondering eyes. The jurors had pounded up the ladder. Kane-Norton, following them, found himself in a low loft, dimly lit, the steam of many wet coats adding to the dimness. From below came the lowing of restless cattle. There was no fireplace, no outlet save a window glazed with old bags, and the square hole they had come through. Kane-Norton, as the reek of farmer and wet frieze coat met him, tried to back; he was borne onwards by a fiery doctor behind him. Some voice remarked that only jurors were admitted, but Doyle, from the door, overbore this with the remark that they were only strange Englishmen who had never seen an Irish corpse before, and were anxious to report on it for the papers.

Something still lay on a mattress in the far corner, a ragged quilt thrown across it. A voice commanded silence, the jurors gathered, and the voice said that Patrick Maddigan had been found dead....

What was that? A crackling, tearing sound f Kane-Norton felt the world giving way beneath him. A wet arm, its owner shrieking with terror, slid round his neck; his arms, wildly seeking safety, clutched another shrieking human being. Then the world gave: they slid into warm, bellowing darkness, a chaos of terrified men, and still more terrified beasts, as a hail of jurors and wood came down on to their quivering backs.

Kane-Norton struck a ramping bullock on its backbone, missed a pointed horn, and then lay supine in what felt like a manure-heap—Irish cow-houses are seldom cleaned. He could not move, partly because a heavy juror lay moaning across his legs, partly because he was afraid of the trampling hoofs all round him.

To the day of his death Kane-Norton will never cease to remember those moments on the squelching cow-house floor, with the great beasts all round and the shower of jurors and of splintered boards continuing. A fat bullock is at all times a rampant animal. A succession of hearty thwacks on their backs made them nearly mad; they rent the air with their furious roars. From the murky darkness he lay in he could see the void, lighter space above, the edges where the floor had given way, and one corner, propped up by a support, still standing. Bellows, curses, groans, made a melee indescribable; the dusty air quivered to the noise.

'God in hivin I are we all dead min this minute?' 'Sthand aisy, ye son o' a horned divil! Haven't ye thrampled the life out of me?' 'Mike Spillane, sthop sthirrin': don't ye see the baste is lookin' to horn ye?' 'Me God! I'm above on this fellow's back, an he leppin like a throut!' Then, from a nervous juror: 'Och, holy Powers! is the dacent corpse down wid us? Hivins above I but I think I feels it adjacent.'

It seemed hours to them before there was a rattle at the closed door and they knew that rescue was at hand.

To the day of his death the Boy says he will never forget the moment when he felt the floor give way and he leapt for sweet safety to the doorpost, Dick Doyle before him. In their hurry they overturned a burly member of the R.I. C. just coming up; this gentleman went bump, bump down the ladder in a sitting posture, his hands clutching the air, and sat at the bottom with a wild expression of surprise on his face. Clinging to the jamb of the door, the Boy saw the boards bend and break, heard the tear and crackle, saw the murky cloud of dust, and the jury vanish—a crowd of

writhing, howling figures—into the bellowing darkness beneath. As his eyes grew accustomed to the darkness, he peered down to see a vision of tossing horned heads and dark figures in the space below. He heard the speeches I have mentioned, together with a ' My God! where have I come to?' in crisp Saxon accents, and occasionally a muffled ' Damn!' evidently emanating from Travers.

Then the Boy rushed down the ladder, to be engulfed in a wave of police and other helpers tearing towards the cow-house door.

'Are ye all dead within there?' asked an anxious voice as they battered at the door. 'An' the masther within himself, an' no one but himself an' the corpse ever havin' the keys.' Here someone suggested 'seeing if the corpse would have them lyin' in his pockets,' but the speaker was overruled. 'Bate the dour down, Pat Murphy! put yer shoulder to it, man! Glory be to God above 1 listen to the bastes roarin' an' the jury squallin'. An' isn't it a terrible thing to think of poor Pat, dacent b'y as he always was, to be thrated in this way, an' he dead an' all. 'Twas an ill strhoke on the head he got, to be flung down wid thim cattle, an' the master havin' thim locked in to be out of the way of the dogs. Howld, man! the corpse is aisy above; sure, the corner of floor he shlep on was held up wid a bit of sthick unther it.'

At this moment the door was burst open. Jurors lay everywhere, huddled against the walls, crouching on the earth, clinging to the maddened bullocks. One man held a beast by the horns; another embraced a pair of stamping legs. Between two raging animals lay a spot of what had once been pink, half covered in oozy mire, a fat farmer across it. It groaned, stirred, and feebly put up its eyeglass, and they knew that it was Kane-Norton. His reason seemed on the point of tottering as he struggled to his feet. His coat was stained to a dull purple; his hat was rescued from a lively hoof, round which it had been festooned.

Then from the hayrack came the

voice of Travers, entreating to be helped down; but he, at least, was clean.

There is honour for ever to Dick Doyle, in that he did not laugt as they helped Travers down from his elevated position and KaneNorton staggered rather than walked towards the door. He cast one awful glance at the splintered loft above; he walked through the jurors, who were wildly recounting their experiences to a sympathetic audience of policemen and farm hands.

'Hadn't I wan hoof in me eye, God's thruth in it, an' two of thim mad divils hornin' me in the back—God's marcy I'm not dead this minute! An' a plank sthruck me an' I fallin'. Toomey an' meself fell adjacent, an' only I see the horns below me, an' turned in the air I was done'

'Begor, ye'd think the divil himself was in it!' The nervous juror crossed himself fervently. ''Twas a quare thing to occur, an' we goin' quiet-like to look at him.'

The coroner here remarked cheerily that'if there was anyone else dead, they might as well come forward, an' let him make one job of it; an' if they were all alive, they might as well lay down some planks an' go an' attind to the corpse that stayed sinsible above—God rest his sowl!'

Kane-Norton reached the door, cleaving his path through the sea of jurors, and—his troubles were not over. In his agitated mind he hoped, at least, to go out into the dimness of the snowstorm; but the treacherous sky had cleared, the storm-cloud was rolling westwards, the cold blue sky was clear and sun-lit. Out into the spotless yard, veiled in dazzling white, came the whole hunt, riding hopefully to look for another fox, heedless of the new cloud which was rolling up behind them. As, merged in a wave of jurors and police, Kane-Norton reached the door, they met him. He struggled to look as if he did not belong to the dishevelled, dirty crowd—vainly. He was a companion in misfortune, and as such they made a comrade of him. The hunt drew up amazed, wondering what had happened, just as one friendly policeman rubbed the purple mire into

fresh streaks on the pink coat, and a still more friendly juror handed him the remains of his hat, with the remark that ''twas ruined entirely, but if he got a bit of a suggawn from wan of the min, and tied it on wid it, 'twould sarve to keep the cold from his head, anyhow.'

The hunt looked, they listened, they laughed —long and heartlessly— pulling up their horses to listen to the tale of the fallen floor—till the fresh snow-shower, creeping up, came down to remind them that hunting for that day was a hopeless thing.

Miss Maguire looked; she met Kane-Norton's eye, and she turned away quickly, but he saw her shoulders shake. Travers was festooned with hay, and came in for some ridicule, but, as I have said before, he was not fresh from five minutes' sojourn in a cow's bed, with a heavy farmer to squash him down into it

Kane-Norton rushed for his horse, and the miles fell fast behind him as he galloped homewards. Fortunately for Hannah Anne's personal safety, she was stricken dumb from amazement, and proffered no immediate remark on his appearance as she opened the door for him. He fled past her to his room. One thought rankled above all the others in Kane-Norton's mind—a thought which he tried to dismiss as unworthy: 'Could Doyle have meant—could he have known when he led them across to see the inquest—that the floor of the loft was too rotten to bear a crowd?'

If Kane-Norton had heard the remark made with a certain dry satisfaction by that gentleman's fireside on the night of the snowy day, it might have enlightened him. It was to the effect that, 'faith, he always knew the old floor wanted patching, but he never dreamt 'twould do him the turn of putting the English dandy down among the cows!' i CHAPTER IX TREATING CHIEFLY OF THE DEAD

'AN" will I carry him out on the road?' asked Mike, the youth who in bygone days had 'cared' Murphy's pony, to say nothing of his pigs, as he put a saddle on Kane-Norton's big hunter.

Kane-Norton never lost an opportunity of trying to improve humanity, and

especially his own servants: he explained at some length that it was quite impossible for Mike to carry the horse anywhere; that the horse, in fact, would carry him, and the sooner he (Mike) dropped such effete and meaningless expressions, the better for all concerned. Mike listened in silence, with the peculiar look, half cunning, half stupidity, which is so annoying to see on an Irish face.

'But, sure,' he remarked, evidently bewildered and turning to the Boy, ' what does he mane at all, at all? Divil a turn this horse iver takes me but where I wants to go, an' he sayin' he could carry me where he'd like.'

The Boy remarked that Mr. Norton was merely trying to show him the correct way of saying things.

'To say things, is it?' Patsey led the horse out, dived for the stirrup, and landed in the saddle. 'An' where will I carry him to, sir?' he inquired, as one who means to have an answer.

'Exercise him on the road to-day,' said KaneNorton, coldly furious, disturbed by the Boy's giggles.

'I wonder you've not given it up by this time, Nor,' he said.

'But it's not sense—it's not grammar,' said Kane-Norton.

'And they're not English—it's Irish grammar,' said the Boy.

'Irish humbug!' observed Kane-Norton crossly.

They strolled across the dirty street to the lodgings, and the Boy, rescuing the hunt card from its dusty nest on the mantelshelf—Hannah Anne generally gave it a 'schlap with the dusther for Sundays'—studied the meets with troubled eyes.

'Friday—Knockadoun,' he said. 'Query for you, Nor: what does Knock mean? Every place is a Knock or a Kill. Now, what's to be done? This place is on the outer edge of the world. I hear we can train down, get within reasonable distance, eight miles or so—but, so far as I can see, the only way to get back is to start three days before the meet.'

'Dear me!' said Kane-Norton, taking it literally as usual. 'Isn't that a little Irish?'

'And am not I a little Irish?' retorted the Boy pleasantly. 'This is a new meet. Doyle tells me that it is outside everyone's country. Some fellow died down there, and the son wrote to Knox thanking him for something he said he would lend for the funeral, and adding in the same breath that he'd seen foxes in the wood, that they were taking his ducks, and they'd better come to look for them. So much for his grief for his father.'

Anything to do with corpses was bitter memory to Kane-Norton. He shuddered.

'Anyhow, we'll chance getting back,' said the Boy. 'Nor, you're going out; tell Mike to

"carry " the horses to the train in the morning, and you'd better go up to your friend the stationmaster and engage a box. We can camp out somewhere if we can't get back. Never do to miss a hunt. The season's growing old.'

So the morning saw them rumbling out into the country. It was one of the soft days of an Irish winter, with pearly-tinted clouds floating in a sky of liquid blue. The hills were greenish-gray, flecked sharply with cloud shadows and golden lights, deepening to brown at their heathery summits. The wind, nosing softly over the land, was westerly, a caress in its touch. They ran through the level green fields—their dream country—stopping with jerks at small stations, where they picked up various sportsmen, past a sluggish river, crawling between muddy banks, and on till civilization seemed far behind, and the train ran between hummocky, craggy fields, fenced altogether with formidable stone walls.

They were bundled out at length, unboxing their horses on the platform of Ballymurphy Station. Then they pounded out into the lonely country, a jog of eight miles before them. Knox, who had tempted them down, acted as guide, twisting and turning through narrow roads. It was a small field. Undipped horses in rusty snaffles sidled and ramped along, their heels unpleasantly active. A couple of girls whom they had never seen out before bumped amongst the crowd, riding in strange brown saddles with arrangements made for carrying a great deal of luggage on the off-side, and clad in habits which suggested petticoats under their many folds. They talked in accents which to Kane-Norton, even after several months' sojourn in the county, were unintelligible.

Kane-Norton rode by Miss Maguire, who had come down in the train with them, and as their guide took them across a field Travers and the Boy ranged up alongside. Then, possibly because of the invitation which had originated this meet, the conversation turned on the people and their dead. Kane-Norton grew pink; he recalled the jury and the cowshed. Miss Maguire observed that he had been treated badly in his one experience of wakes and such things, and she distinctly bit off a chuckle.

'Have you heard of the funeral from Caragh Workhouse last week?' asked Doyle, ranging up and joining in the conversation, ' where they were all strolling off to the graveyard, and the men with the coffin were remarking that it was a bit light, when after them, helter-skelter, came one of the workhouse officials, shouting out that they'd forgotten the corpse; 'twas within still, and they had to go back to fetch it.'

'Dear me,' said Kane-Norton with a shudder, 'what a land!'

'Next to a wedding, and possibly before it, there's no doubt they enjoy a funeral,' said Miss Maguire thoughtfully. 'I've had a horror of such things all my life, because, when I was a child, my nurse took me to a wake. I can see the whole thing yet: the dead man's face, the candles—it was ghastly!' She shivered. 'Here we are at last.'

A long hillside with patches of trees topping it—trees with an undergrowth of tangled bramble and stunted thorn, good cover for a fox. They all looked at it anxiously, for if it was blank there was a long jog back to the next place they could draw—the whole meet was a chance of sport.

The excited owner of the land came tumbling up the hill before them, telling Knox and Sir Ralph, in wild whispers, that the ' schamers were both surely within, and that he and his son, little Danny, crep' in lasht night in the darkenin" an' sthopped every mortial hole in the place.'

They all pulled up. As far as eye could reach rolled the desolate country, rise after rise, with the ragged gray wall fringes, their crop of crags, or stunted thorn-bushes. Beyond the craggy land away to the left the fields were green and clear. Here and there a patch of trees marked a dwelling-place, but they were few to see. To the left a great belt of trees broke the sky-line; to the right, gleaming silver, they could see the Cahir rolling seawards. Topping one stretch of hill, a ruin cut across the landscape—a piece of crumbling wall, gray and lonely, the old narrow window-slits defying in places time which warred with them. Here in old times the robber chiefs had watched for their spoils. The Cahirvally the three men were used to was plate-shaped, rimmed round by hills. This country was limitless, until in the far distance blue mountains showed faintly.

A wave of eager bodies across the grass, a crackle and crash in the undergrowth, a whimper, then a note in covert. Old Melody sprang on the wide stone fence, her face eager, her stern waving; then, putting her nose down, she spoke emphatically. Half a dozen hounds came to her well-known cry. A moment later a fox broke at the upper end of the wood, and stole away towards the craggy country, making for a clump of thorns in the distance.

'We're not here for nothing, then,' said Sir Ralph, as he clapped his hounds on the line.

They all galloped over the hummocky land, stumbling and slipping as the hummocks alternated with slabs and points of stone. It was not a pleasant country to ride over. The walls were big and double; horses went on and off as if they were banks, with a clinking rattle of falling stones. They crossed a road, dipped into a steep bush-grown valley, and out on to another road, hunting slowly.

'What's that?' Travers pointed to a crowd on the road they were coming to.

'It's—yes, a funeral,' said the master,

who was beside him, 'and hounds hunting right up to it.'

A wild yell bore down-wind to them. A dark figure appeared, sharply outlined against the pale sky, on a fence. The words reached them: 'He's away! Past here! Down by the thorn-bush; then he twisted, making back!'

They could bury a man any day, but a hunt was a novelty down here. One of the priests, who had just ridden over, was the 'tallyer' of their fox. His mourning-bands floated out on the breeze; he held his horse by the bridle. The hearse waited, empty, on the road by the house as they came up. A mourner flung himself on a shaggy pony, and urged it madly at a stone gap into the field; its reluctance to jump was forcibly overcome by other mourners armed with thick sticks. 'Success!' they yelled, as the woolly horse shattered the gap and the hunt came tearing up.

With hasty words, reeking of whisky, they directed the master onwards, referring specially to Father Doolan, ' who was just coming along, whin the fox crossed under his very nose.'

His white weepers waving, Father Doolan bundled off the wall he stood on, and rushed down the field on the line the fox had taken.

'There 'tis! there 'tis!' he cried enthusiastically, watching the hounds. 'My! my! Tear an' ages! Isn't it the cruel pity that I must go back to bury the man, an' this horse I have here the finest lepper ye ever clapped yer eyes on?'

'Have they got no feeling—no respect—for anything?' muttered Kane-Norton, who, still sore on the subject of corpses, had ridden slowly and with uncovered head through the funeral cortege, getting a glimpse of the coffin halfway out the door, where the bearers had hastily set it down.

James Heffernan, the owner of the wood, met them as he made his breathless way to the funeral, and gave a fresh word of the fox.

So far as hunting went, it was a satisfactory morning, but of excitement or pleasure there was none. They wound round and round in a weary track, slipping over crags, stumbling over heaps, sliding down bush-grown hills, scrambling up, and always with the rattle of falling stones in their ears, as the gaps in the oft-crossed walls grew wider.

The morning waned. As they topped the rises they could see the funeral in the bare graveyard, close to the gray stone chapel, and after a time stragglers from it began to join the hunt

The master, solicitous, inquired if they had given offence by riding so close to the dead, and was heartily reassured by a burly redwhiskered man, who said he was first cousin to the corpse, and evidently held himself to be an authority.

'Wasn't Hickey a man who rode to the dogs himself?' he said, his voice mellow from potations. 'Isn't it the fine sportin' funeral he'd had—God rest his soul! 'Twas a proud man he'd be the day, if he could know.' He cast an eye towards the graveyard, as if considering the possibility of sending a message. 'Faith, one 'd think he settled it,' he concluded.

'Ireland! Ireland!' muttered Travers, overhearing.

The clouds were beginning to put a soft belt round the horizon, when at last the fox found an unstopped hole, and left the hounds baying crossly at the mouth, looking for human assistance; they could do no more.

There seemed nothing for it but a jog back to Goleen, many miles away, when Heffernan, heated, and with a reek of fiery whisky in his breath, bore hurriedly down on them. 'They had put one fox away,' he told them, 'but surely to goodness the second fellow never made a sthir, but was lyin' above yit.' Another wander round the crags did not sound promising, but neither did an eight-mile jog. They moved again to the wood on the hill.

They gathered at the same corner, longing for a gallop over the stretch of green fields on the left. The Cahir was leaden-coloured now, shadowed by the clouds which were hurrying up.

'I'm tired,' Miss Maguire yawned; 'hillclimbing doesn't agree with me.'

Kane-Norton observed languidly that it was a country for goats, and not horses. The velvety-eyed girl, never far away from his side, agreed with him heartily, looking at her young horse's battered legs.

'Tally-ho!' came from the Boy in a bloodcurdling whisper.

Right under their feet broke a big fox, and set his mask for the distant river. He distanced a yelling cur-dog, dodged the wildly-cheering portion of the funeral party who saw him, lobbed over a wall, and stole up the field beyond.

'Go-one away! go-one away!' One small red body, and half a hundred people half wild with excitement because it was in their sight.

Hounds poured out of covert and went away like a flash. Scent, the mysterious, was good enough now. The crags were left behind; the going rang light under the horses' feet as they thudded down the first slope and flung a low stone wall behind.

It was a line to dream of for anyone who liked a gallop which partook of the nature of a steeplechase. There was nothing to stop hounds or horse, and after a few fields slow horses dropped back. The pace was something to remember. When they had galloped for about twenty minutes it steadied, but the hunt poured on, up and down the sloping pastures, over wall after wall, double or single. On and on, the river shining nearer as they topped the hills, vanishing as they sank into the hollow.

The pace steadied again; hounds were brought to their noses more than once. They ran through a belt of trees, and came out on to a stretch of low ground crossed by boggy drains. A cloud of silver spray went up as the pack dropped into the first one. Holding horses together through the moist churning earth, a lift, a touch of spur or whip, and over, with a sensation of hind-legs slipping and a vision of cool, dark water beneath—a vision which became reality to some. Hearts which were soft turned back. As those who had got over the drains crept through a gap in a built wall, fencing the road beyond the bog, the field had dwindled sadly.

The evening darkened, and the long

hunt drifted on. Tired horses came with a grunt over the walls, their strong limbs moving stiffly with the laboured gallop of a blown horse. Even Ould Tim chanced his fences badly more than once. The tale of big knees for the morning would be a large one.

They were close to the river, getting into the deep holding pasture bordering its banks, when hounds swung sharply to the left, and headed for the belt of trees looming blackly in the failing light. They had been running for two hours, and it was five o'clock. Eight people still kept with the hounds: the three Englishmen, the master, Miss Maguire, Miss Martin, Doyle, and a man whose name they did not know, The *test* had vanished.

They landed with a scramble into a narrow road, to be confronted by a wide patch of yellow bogland, cut across by deep brown peat where turf had been taken away and the stagnant water lay blackly. The evening wind rustled mournfully amongst the long coarse grass. Hounds flung up puzzled heads, then took up the line right across the bog. The road ran flatly, vanishing like a streak in the distance. There was not a soul within sight. A cart-track ran beside the bog towards a stony little hill, and Travers, as Sir Ralph spurred his tired horse through the soft earth, held up a warning hand.

'Wait,' he said; 'he may be to ground there. See which way they turn. It would be madness to try to ride the bog in this light and with the horses dead beat."

'Who-hoop! who-hoop!' reached them just as he spoke. The fox had beaten them; he was to ground in the craggy rise. They stood watching in the twilight, jumping off their tired horses, which stood with heads down and heaving flanks. Miss Maguire jumped off, too, leading her gray down to a pool near the side of the track. 'I wonder where we are,' she said in a tired voice. 'It's dark, and I have to get back to Inagh; my trap is there.'

Silence answered her—silence and the wind rustling through the reeds. Dark clouds spread out rapidly across the sky. The west was barred with scar-

let and amber. Then Travers supposed carelessly that Sir Ralph and the others knew their way. He watched the hill, wondering why they did not come back. They had all disappeared. He went on wondering; the stony hill showed no signs of life, and when at last they went over to it, there was not a horse or hound within sight: they had vanished into the gray evening.

Someone suggested following the tracks, which were deeply marked on the boggy earth, but as there were two boggy roads, and it was very dark, this seemed impossible. They returned to the road. One streak ran into the barred west, so the other must be theirs. They started along it, the horses quickly gathering the fact that no one knew where they were going to, and moving listlessly, their ears back. The road was unfenced save for the great cuts at either side, where a stumble might land you over the crumbling edges. The gleam of the dead sun flung a rusty gleam over the brown turf, a tinge of copper in the water; then it purpled, faded, and the bog grew cold and black.

Sheila Maguire shivered; her listless figure showed how tired she was.

The bog ended after a mile or so in a maze of cross-roads. They stopped. 'We are at the world's end,' said the girl—' not a house anywhere. We may take this road and find ourselves at the Cahir, or miles away from where we want to go to.' Her ordinary hard, masculine manner was merged in fatigue. She was a tired woman, and she showed it. 'Well?' she said, pointing with her whip at the three roads. The Boy gathered Ould Tim together, and, remarking that, anyhow, a road must lead somewhere, and the bog would make a cold camping-ground, took the middle one.

They jogged on. Sometimes it was dark; at times a scudding moon, racing with the scudding clouds, lit them on their way. The walls slid past in interminable array; the twisting road seemed endless.

'A light at last!' Travers pointed to a little pin-point of brightness raying the gloom. 'We'll get a drink for the horses somehow, if we have to steal it, and

some tea for you.' He trotted on, his horse's hoofs ringing, its quarters growing quickly dim.

They followed him slowly till they reached the cottage, and were aware of hurried words spoken in horrified tones, then of a woman's figure, strangely tidy, outlined in the yellow gleam from the door. The room was also strangely tidy, and with an array of glasses on a centre table, flanked by plates of sugared biscuits. The whole looked cosy in the mingled light of cheap paraffin candles and turf. The array of dirty packages in the window marked the fact that it was a little shop.

'I'll give ye tay, sir, an' welcome; there's lashins of flour for the horses, but ye see, ye see'

The Boy pressed in behind Travers, and saw a big bed with a still figure lying on it, its composed face waxy white in the light of the tall candles which flared at head and foot. A girl sat by the fire, her head in her hands. The Boy stepped out quickly, blocking the doorway. The two girls saw none of these things. He remembered what Miss Maguire had said that morning.

'You can'l come in,' he said; 'there's someone ilV Then, as they groaned, his eye fell on a cow-house at the back. 'We'll go in there," he said positively; 'warm for the horses, and I can bring you some tea.'

'1 won't get off'—Miss Maguire had reached the fretful stage—' if I can't go into the house. I'm not going to sit in hay. Is it infectious?'

The Boy blocked the door with his horse, and Kane-Norton was muttering feverishly that all Ireland seemed to be dead.

Infectious? It's a common complaint, but we'll none of us catch it to-night I hope,' said the Boy quietly.

'Well, you wait; I'll ride on slowly,' said the lady.

Travers began to argue. The Boy laid his hand on her bridle and led her to the door of the cow-house. There he ordered her to get off. Somehow, she scarcely knew how, Miss Maguire found herself on the ground.

'But—what am I to do now?' she

said, half whimper, half anger.

'This,' said the Boy tersely.

Kane-Norton's eyeglass dropped. Travers murmured 'Damn!' feebly, for the Boy took the heiress, the lady of importance, under the arms, swung her off her feet as if she had been a baby, and dumped her down into a heap of hay. She might have sprung up, but hay is of a yielding disposition; her body sank as her heels went up, and she only gasped in futile anger.

'There you stay till you get something to eat,' observed the Boy, looking down at her.

'May I ask,' inquired Miss Maguire sharply, striving to struggle out of her doubled-up attitude, 'whether you are a Sandow in disguise?'

'I shouldn't care to stand up to him in a boxing match. He's won a few,' said Travers, leading the horses to the far end of the shed as the Boy clumped off. Kane-Norton was lifting Katie Martin down, and thinking as he did so how deep her eyes looked in the dim light. He would never have thought himself of taking tea in a cow-house, but he was getting past being surprised at anything.

It was indeed a strange tea-party. The men came and went, lifting steaming kettles, toasting bread, spreading butter, declining proffered whisky, always with the knowledge of that silent, waxen-faced watcher on the bed. His widow bustled cheerily, turning the bellows to blow up the fire, hanging the kettle on the black, sooty hook in the wide chimney, talking as she did so in low tones of the corpse, of the wake which she was ready for.

The girl by the fire wept on stonily. She was the dead man's twin sister. The wife would cry later, when there was someone to see her.

They put a lamp on one of the bales in the cow-house to give them a little light, and the two girls drank hot tea and ate thick toast. The Boy kept them company; the other two did not seem hungry. The waxen-faced watcher had damped their appetites.

Tea was eaten to the accompaniment of the horses, freshened by their drinks, champing hay and rattling their bits.

The soft smell of the hay pervaded the air; the lamp flickered down on them; a trickle of light fell across the yard outside from the tiny sealed window of the cottage.

'It's just as good as getting in,' remarked Miss Maguire, snuggling into the warmth of the hay. 'Poor woman! Is that man very sick? Irish though I am, as I told you this morning, I hate anything to do with death. I shudder when I think of Mrs. Gleeson's tea at Moyastra. They were having an inquest there on one of her men who had died suddenly, when they heard that a lot of the hunting people were coming in. Old Mrs. Gleeson wailed, declaring that she would be ruined if the men came and found her having an inquest in the room they took tea in. So she cajoled the jury, bundled the corpse under the sofa, and gave all those men tea in that room. If I'd been one of those people, I'd never have forgotten it.'

Kane-Norton shuddered, thinking of the watcher inside. He was not strong-minded; he ate no tea.

They went out at length into the chill, dim evening. Already some few people were gathering for the wake; it was high time to be off. Gleaning directions for their road, they mounted. Glasses chinked inside, and a warm whiff of bad whisky drifted out to them.

All might have been well, but, moved to fervent gratitude by the pile of silver they left her, the widow rushed out, and, grasping Miss Maguire's horse by the head, poured out due apologies for the presence of the corpse which had ' kep' such a gran' lady from the warm of the fireside. Indade, if Paddy himself was there, he'd lose his life to see ye takin' tay in the cow-shed. Proud he'd have been to have ye come in now, but their honours said you'd be fearsome, and had no wish for the dead.'

'Do you mean to say,' asked Miss Maguire, in tones of sick horror, 'that there is a corpse in that house? And I had tea, and you made toast, from there, and—oh!'

She rode on, shuddering.

The two elder men looked at the Boy, as much as to say:' There, we told you

so; you've done harm!'

'Poor soul! he couldn't hurt you,' said the Boy, in answer to her fiery glance. 'You were dead beat, and had to have something!'

'You took me off; you put me in!' she said. 'You made me take tea! I'll never forgive it!'

The others breathed heavily; fortunately, it was the Boy she was annoyed with.

'I—did,' said the Boy placidly. «What's more, if it happened over again, and we met a house with two dead people in it, I'd do it again. Make up your mind to that.'

He smote Ould Tim softly on the neck and broke into a jog.

'Oh!' said the lady blankly. He could not see her face.

The ride to Inagh was nightmare-like. Endless roads, endless asking and arguing, endless trotting here and there up to houses whose lights marked them in the dimness. The horses stumbled along, conversation died a weary, lingering death, and they moved on in silence. The night wind sobbed and moaned behind them, heavy with the coming rain; the dim, bare country stretched at either side. It was nearly eight when they crossed a noisy river, running ghostly white as it foamed over a weir close to the bridge, and clattered up the steep, stony street of Inagh village, where Miss Maguire had left her trap, and where they left their horses for the night. It did not comfort them to hear that the hounds had passed through some hours before.

After a meal of eggs and bacon, they found a night train to take them back to Cahirvally.

The bright fire in the lodgings, the array of bottles laid out by Hannah Anne, were almost homelike.

'There is one thing,' observed Kane-Norton as he mixed hot punch and resuscitated his tired frame with the steaming mixture, ' that I hope I shall never be in Ireland.'

'What's that?' asked the Boy languidly.

'A corpse,' said Kane-Norton with due solemnity.

CHAPTER X 4 A SOUTHERLY WIND AND A CLOUDY SKY'

To be accurate, it was a westerly wind, light clouds scudding across the sky, the balmy, fresh breath of spring in the air. The snow had vanished; nothing lasts in Ireland, from the money in the men's pockets down to the weather. It freezes, the ponds wrinkle, skates are oiled, some few venture on the ice—which lets them in, as a rule—then it thaws again. It rains, and by the time we have settled down for a wet day the clouds are breaking, and a pale sun comes out to mock at us for having stayed in.

The land is a mighty child, for ever at play with the elements, and her people are children also, from their birth to the day when the grave yawns for them. Irresponsible, impressionable, seldom able to see clearly, swayed by every brazen-tongued orator, who shall blame them for the foolish things they do?

The willow buds were swelling; the earth waked. The tillers of the soil were busy pigmies on her wide bosom; year by year she had given, now she was ready to give again.

All this, and the most perfect country in the world stretching all round, billowing slopes of grass to the foot of the purpling hills, and hounds working through a gorse covert.

The whips stood motionless at either corner; the field grouped expectantly, listening for a whimper, brave hearts hoping for the sound, faint hearts hoping for none—for to get away from Dullane one must jump; it was no place for shirkers.

Miss Maguire stood near the covert, her big black standing patiently, with cocked ears and watchful eyes on the rustling gorse. The crowd near chanced to hold the Boy, and he bore down on her more than once, mounted on a ramping, raking bay and sorely disturbing her peace.

'What on earth are you riding that thing for?' she asked at length, as the bay wheeled, bumping her. 'It's—no—yes, it *is* Dollie McCarthy's Clear the Way.'

'Just so,' said the Boy, giving the beast a job in the mouth, and then sitting down to its fretful plunge; 'she lent it to me to get it fit— to get me fitted for a coffin, did you say? Oh no; both mine are laid up, worse luck! and then she told me she wanted it made fit for the Point-to-Point.'

'You ought not to attempt to ride a horse of that description,' said Miss Maguire severely. 'Let Tommy, her brother, ride it himself if she wants to run it; but, good man as he is, he won't try it. It's a brute, with the legs of a hare—but never your horse. Now, for next year for you'

'For me there is no next year,' said the Boy, sighing. He ceased, trying to keep his wild mount quiet, and in answer she stood for a moment peacefully. 'Those others will be here again'—he looked at her to see if she blushed —' but I—well, one can't hunt on credit.'

'You won't come back again, then?' Her eyes were fixed on the covert.

'Worse luck, no!' ('No chance of an invitation for me,' thought the Boy.)

He then proceeded to explain how very little money he had that he could not touch, and how all that he could touch had melted rapidly down to the very last legacy. Also he told her, the soft west wind chiming in with his melancholy, how his dream of making his winter's expenses by his horses this year in Ireland had vanished also, for when the time came he could not resist the temptation of riding trained screws. Travers would possibly sell his horse well in England if he wanted to— the Boy looked again for another blush— who would give him even as much as he originally paid for Ould Tim? and the gray had gone wrong.

There was, so far, no whimper in the gorse; it was long and thick. Miss Maguire listened to him attentively. They did not often have so long a conversation, but since the affair of Andy Magrath and his wife's fortune a certain good fellowship, masked by much bickering, had sprung up between them.

'Foolish,' she said—' Foolish!' yet something softened her face. 'You'd like to come here again, then?' she asked briefly.

'Like it?' Memories gushed up in the Boy's heart—memories of happy gallops; of springy turf thudding under eager, iron-shod hoofs; of fences flung behind while the pack strained in front; of the hopes and sorrows and fresh hopes which weld men's hearts to hunting. He thought, too, of the brown bogs, the gorsy hillsides, the happy evenings with water squelching in wet boots, and a gun growing heavy in the tired walks homewards, Mickey, ever voluble, trotting by his side, and other people's birds and beasts in the bag. Something, some stir in his blood, took his thoughts back to Norah and Martin in their little cabin on the bare, sunny hillside. Ireland can tune herself better to sorrow than joy; the wind rustling through the thorns seemed to sigh in sympathy with him.

His cheek flushed. 'Like it? I think I'm born to the place; my mother was Irish, y' know. P'raps some day, when I've made a fortune, I'll come back and ride over it all again;' but his brow grew heavier. 'Some day' is a sad word to careless youth. At twenty-five, who can imagine thirty-five knowing how to enjoy life? Ould Tim would be dead then, eaten, in all probability, by the hounds he had strained his gallant limbs to follow. Cahirvally would have changed, would have forgotten the Boy.

He looked at the waiting crowd— Doyle, wrapped round by other Doyles, laying down the law as to which way the fox would break, when they found him. Donovan Moore, seeming one with his well-bred brown mare, standing close to the covert, waiting for the first note. Lean, grumpy, he was still a sportsman to his heart's core, and one of the best men to hounds in Ireland. He had no quarrel with the Boy, and in his way had been almost kind to him, flinging out short words of advice, which the Boy tried to follow. Nay, once when the Boy almost jumped on him, treading his reins into the earth, he had actually forborne strong language, merely saying with a backward look at the big bank: 'Go on, youngster! it's your heart brought you here.'

The four Miss Clancys were there, all mounted, from the eldest on her hunter— Martin, grumpy and sad, in attendance—down to the youngest, screwed into her mother's old saddle, on the patient half-clipped cart-pony. They belonged to the race of sportswomen who rode hard and straight, but who looked on hounds as mere necessary aids to a pleasure, and who marked the joys of their gallops by the relative positions they occupied to other habits. Moreover, if a man fell, it was not unlikely that the eldest Miss Clancy would jump on him. There were the Caseys, one drunk, one sober, on a fresh pair of young horses; the fringe of country people all round, their low-pitched, blurring voices coming plainly to him. 'Is he widin?' 'Widin, man! didn't he whip two docks from the widow Brady lasht night? an' Dinny Brady seen him runnin' home so as to ate thim at his aise. ' 'Divil a dog sphoke to him yit, thin!' 'For why? the schamer's lyin' close.' 'I tell ye he isn't in it at all.' 'Yerra, don't be blatherin'; didn't James here see a flock of foxes skhelpin' in from Graigue lasht evenin'?' 'Whisht 1 isn't that a dog talkin' now?'

The Boy looked; he listened; and he felt his heart go out to them. England was a place to stay in; Ireland, with her gray skies and her desolation, her quick tongues and her friendly hearts—Ireland was his home. It called to him, and he might not answer. He had been born far away under brassy Eastern skies. Who might say what longing his Irish mother had felt, as she panted out her life under the swinging punkah, for the pearly heavens, the cool sweet winds of her native land.

Sheila Maguire's voice, asking him where he meant to go to, roused him.

'Where '—the Boy waved a vague hand; young people always take a certain pleasure in their sorrows, their first-born children of trouble —' where does the drift go to? The Cape— West Africa—Australia—where all the other ne'er-do-weels get to, who have been brought up in the mistaken idea that they have money. I'll never starve; and p'raps'—his face brightened—' I've another brace of aunts, and when the Lord takes a fancy to one of thim— I quote Hannah Anne—p'raps I may find money for another winter's hunting here.'

Farther down the field, Kane-Norton was standing by the little horse-breaker with the pathetic eyes. She had not tried to sell him any more horses. But their acquaintance had ripened, and she showed such palpable admiration of his fine personality that, when he was not in close attendance on Miss Maguire, he let the light of his favour fall on her.

It was hard to resist the open admiration ol those big velvety eyes and flushing cheeks. It was pleasant especially to Kane-Norton to knowthat every word he let fall was a verbal diamond or pearl—that England, his birthplace, was regarded as a mystic country full of unknown joys. There were even moments when he fell to thinking how pretty the little girl would look in garments of another cut, and how many eyes would turn to look at her in the Park on Sundays.

Travers and he had come to recognise the fact that they were rivals by now, but they took it good-temperedly—let the race fall to the strongest. Neither could say he was more favoured than the other. The 'orphint'— how long ago that day seemed when Maddigan had so described her!—smiled on them both impartially. They were constantly out there. Doyle and Moore had in consequence, after an enmity of years, become fast friends, and spent their lives in trying to jostle the Englishmen out hunting. When, after many years, they had decided to resign the joys of bachelordom, it was hard to have the ground struck from under their feet by two strangers.

Kane-Norton taught the lady cunning strokes at billiards. Travers took his weight down by playing ping-pong, and groping red-faced for little white balls, which sped like live things into corners.

The men looked, they hinted, but they had not spoken, and who might say? The big white house, the big, fair-skinned girl, the right to ride for ever over the grass land— these things grew more desirable daily as the months slipped by. Now February was upon them, and decision stared them in the face.

Miss Maguire bore another bump — with some impatience; then, in tones of asperity, she recommenced her argument. The mare was not fit for the Boy to ride; he was raw, rough; only an artist could possibly get him across a country. 'Look here,' she added, 'my groom is over there, riding a four-year-old of mine; he's an absolutely perfect performer. You can —you can—change on to him.'

She said it slowly, as if with an effort, and the Boy was quick to note this. He shook his head decidedly. His voice was stiff. He would on no account take her youngster; besides, he had promised Dollie McCarthy

Miss Maguire shot a vicious glance through the crowd, its object a lumpy, good-looking girl in a light-blue habit.

'And then, you see, I ride so badly,' went on the Boy.

'It's just because you ride so badly that I am offering you my horse/ said the heiress sharply.

'Quarrelling with the Boy as per usual?' said Travers, edging up through the crowd. There was a whimper now in the gorse.

'Trying, endeavouring to make him see, to make him sensible. Now, will you take my horse, Mr. Rivers?'

'Very kind of you, but I will *not,*' said the Boy haughtily. 'Dollie McCarthy'

Sheila Maguire muttered something to the effect that, if he was bent on killing himself for Miss McCarthy's sake, it was no business of hers, and turned a cross young profile to them. Travers shook a dissatisfied head; these constant quarrels with the Boy, he felt sure, must to a certain extent embitter the lady against them. He looked at the Boy angrily; he tried to work round the girl's displeased back to say something soothing. At that moment the fox broke.

Right along the field in front of them, stealing along with a whisk of his brush as he slipped over the first fence; an old customer who knew his point and meant to get there. Several impetuous spirits among the field flung themselves hotly on the line, and only pulled up sullenly as the master came tearing up, with a sweet-toned intimation that, if they cared to go on, he'd no doubt that he could take his useless hounds home. Then with a crash hounds poured out through the hedge round the gorse; noses to earth, they took up the line. Old Melody spoke; they flew to her, and were away, a dappled mass of eager, wistful faces, of straining bodies, a wave of white and tan pouring over a low green bank.

'Now gallop over them if you're able. You set of spoil-sports!' grunted Sir Ralph as he set his horse going.

Life is a weary thing, but it has its compensations. That run, for those who saw it, was one of them.

They bent sharply to the left as they started, then an equally sharp turn to the right, hounds driving ahead on a burning scent, field upon field of grass land in front. Fences big but honest, needing a bold horse to get over them.

Miss Maguire took her place to the right of the hounds, the Boy near her; Travers and Kane-Norton close at hand. I say the Boy took his place; I should say that Clear the Way took hers. With her awkward nose stuck straight in the air, her mouth wide open, she rushed full speed at the fences, checked herself in the last stride, and with a wild slip and struggle reached the next field; nothing but her activity saving her. On and off, on and off, went Miss Maguire's big bay, bold one moment, cautious the next, creeping down a drop, flinging a wide drain behind him, changing like a pony on a razor-topped bank, flying a wall. The air rushed in their faces; the thunder of hoofs on turf rang behind; the pack strained in front. Was there anything like it on earth? The Boy's heart danced; his cheeks were scarlet. Who thought of next year now? that was to come—this was

If Clear the Way did blunder at her fences, she could gallop; there was time, thought the Boy optimistically, to fall and get up again once or twice. He swung her recklessly at a high narrow bank; she swerved, jumped sideways, and landed in a heap outside. The Boy sat on many portions of her body, but

they did not part company. Merrylass slipped over, flicking the fence with her active heels. Then came a moment's check—a needed one; horses were panting.

Miss Maguire landed close by the Boy, just as he had tried to turn his mare, and had succeeded, instead, in colliding with the whip, who looked injured.

'You'll kill yourself,' said the lady sourly.

'Time enough to cry out when you're dead,' remarked the Boy cheerfully.

His hat was on the back of his head, his tie under one ear, there was a scratch on his cheek, and it was doubtful if he had ever been happier in his life.

'Mad, mad 1' said Miss Maguire aloud—' but a sportsman down to his boots,' she added to herself.

Hounds spread out seeking for the line, working quite alone, the master standing still until it was evident that they wanted his help. Then they flashed across a big bank, with a wide grip at the taking-off side, an uncertainty at the landing. Four horses charged it abreast, four pieces of treacherous earth slid under the pressing of hoofs, four people went into the uncertainty outside, which, to judge by the splashing, sounded—wet. Hounds were running like pigeons up the field beyond, but the rest of the field stopped to have a look. The Boy took his wild mare by the head.

'You're certain to fall. Don't try it on that brute!' cried Miss Maguire.

The Boy humped an obstinate back; he was rather cross. He had resented more than he could have believed he would the slur on his riding, which he thought had improved so much; and he was bent on proving to the lady that he was not quite such a duffer as she thought him. He meant, if possible, to keep in front of the good bay horse.

'There's one thing: there are heaps of people to pick me up,' he said thoughtfully, looking at the four men outside; two chasing their horses, two pulling their mounts out of the ditch. He set the mare going fast. She sailed into the air, and cleared the whole thing handsomely, landing with a slight stagger.

'Well, after that we shall have him trying to charge the railway gates,' said the lady, setting her teeth and going at the fence.

It was too humiliating to be left behind by Dollie McCarthy's Clear the Way. Miss Maguire got over with a bad blunder, but no fall.

Across holding land now, horses labouring in it. Out on to a road, the cattle-gap fenced with a stiff piece of timber. The Boy was first at it. The reins flapped on Clear the Way's neck; she was sufficiently blown at the moment to allow of liberties being taken. Fortunately, the stick was rotten, for she never rose an inch, and, somewhat sourly, the Boy heard the thanks of the field ringing in his rear.

Hounds bent to the left; satiny necks were dark with sweat; flanks heaved rapidly. Sir Ralph pointed to a hill, with a fringe of fir-trees clear against the sky-line.

'Our point,' he said. 'It's a Tullanby fox making his way home. We ought to kill him before he gets there.'

It was sound pasture again now; sound banks, where thirty horses might take their places abreast. A perfect line, a perfect land, thought Travers as Merrylass strode on under him, with a thoroughbred's elastic, untiring stride. Looking back, they could see a long tail coming on, the horses rising and falling like mechanical toys in the distance. The pace had told, and there were only about twelve people near hounds, Miss Maguire and the little horse-dealer the only ladies. They ran along the crest of a gorsy hill, hounds working slowly through the thick green growth; the fox had evidently tried the rocks. Then the line ran past a plantation, and the pack poured out of sight into what looked like a ravine.

Dick Doyle appeared to know his way; he rode up on the bank fencing the wood and then disappeared from view.

Horses had to slide on their tails down into a mighty ditch, then climb grunting up the far side. The Boy, riding a little to the left, saw them, and tried to haul Clear the Way round, but she would have none of it. Her nose straight out, she dashed through the trees and sprang on to the bank, and the Boy saw the world disappear into a gorse-grown ravine outside. Those lower down held their breaths. It looked as if it must inevitably be a nasty fall; but the mare hurled herself into the air, and reached the other side—on her head, it was true, with her heels waving over the void, and sending the Boy into a furze-bush. But she got there.

The Boy, who had held on to the reins, came out of his prickly nest, peered down into the depths beneath, watched the hunters crawling up and down through the ditch; then he whistled and remounted. Clear the Way had saved a bad fall cleverly—that was how he put it.

Slowly now, on the failing scent of a tired fox, they worked along towards the hill, with its fringe of dark fir-trees showing plainly.

A yell above them: someone had viewed him. Yes, he was in sight now, creeping with bowed back and drooping brush up the hill. Horses sobbed as they breasted the ascent, their necks white with foam; but they faced their fences as keenly as ever, gathering tired limbs for the spring, as a good hunter will until he drops. The sun gleamed out on them—a fair sight: the pack racing upwards, the pink coats against the green, the long tail of horsemen behind.

The Boy gathered his mare together and raced to the front. He passed Miss Maguire, and was human enough to point to her horse and say ' Done' in a tone of sympathy.

A sudden burst of music from the pack as they dashed from scent to view at racing pace over the firm green fields, with only stone gaps to jump; a turn; another; grinning teeth bared in impotent fury as a gallant fox met his death gallantly, his teeth buried in one of his foes— run down in the open at the end of the run of the season. Moreover, the Boy got the brush; he had gone well throughout, and, to be accurate, having taken hold of Clear the Way, he was quite unable to check her, and was in the middle of the pack when they killed. He got off, sitting down breathlessly on a

bank, his face aglow.

'Oh, what a hunt!' he gasped. 'Good old Clear the Way.'

Her face like a thundercloud, Sheila Maguire pulled up beside him.

'I trust,' she said bitterly, 'that you will never ride that horse again.'

'What?' The Boy turned, his triumph hot upon him.

'She never changed on a bank, she chested timber, she ran away with you over that ravine. You're a danger to yourself—and to everyone else.'

'You're always down on me,' said the Boy in nettled tones, looking at his draggled brush. 'I got here first, at any rate. And, you know, you must have been behind me to have seen all that.'

This was rude, but true. Miss Maguire coloured.

'I shall win the race on her,' went on the Boy.

'And you—you will ride, I suppose, though the girl's own brother won't get on the brute for her?'

Kane-Norton, observing that an altercation was going on, came with his accustomed tact hastily to the rescue. Really, it was too bad of the Boy, straining things as he did. Strange to say, Miss Maguire did not seem to be pleased to see him. She stopped arguing, and rode away moodily, honouring Miss Dollie McCarthy, who had arrived upon the scene and was bubbling over with pride at her mare's success, with a glance which caused that damsel first to colour hotly, and then to put up her hand hastily, first to her hat, and then to her tie, wondering what could be wrong with her personal appearance.

-They were close to Dunmore, and all went back there to tea. It was desirable—oh, undoubtedly desirable— thought Travers, as he handed round plates of buttered toast. Solid, old-fashioned, but what a range of boxes in the yard at the back, what a vista of the perfect country they had ridden over, visible through an opening in the trees! And Travers was in love. Most desirable of all was the girl sitting at the tea-table, with the firelight playing on her fair hair, on her fine, pale skin. She looked tired; she handed the Boy his tea

as if it were a weapon of defence, and Travers sighed. He was fond of the Boy. If the future worked out as he hoped it might, it would grieve him not to be able to be kind to the youngster.

The room, with its old-fashioned chintz coverings, its stiff range of valuable china on the marble mantelshelf, was very homelike. The old grate was brass-rimmed; it was apparent that the heiress was conservative, and cared little for fashion. Here and there some new piece of artistic furniture jostled with the chintz, and seemed to suffer by the comparison. Mrs. Moore, the old chaperon, sat by the fire, principally employing her time in building it up. She had taken charge of Sheila from the day, twenty years ago, when a runaway horse had deprived the child of both mother and father.

They started off in a soft spring twilight, the sky silvery, deepening to blue, bars of amber light on the horizon, a westerly wind crooning in the trees. The hills rose dimly purple and gray above the woods. The Boy looked wistfully through the valley, where the trees had been cut away to give a view of the billowing country, with a streak of river running through it. There was the wood where the Scotch keeper had found him; the man was hanging about now, little dreaming that one of the pinkcoated hunt was his lost poacher. There was the wall he had climbed over. Beyond were the fields which held such happy memories.

'I believe,' he said as to himself, as he swung up on to Clear the Way's uneasy back—Miss McCarthy had wrung her withers more than once—' that I envy Martin and Norah in their little cabin; they can live here, anyhow.'

'1 believe,' said Miss Maguire in tired tones into Clear the Way's mane— he had not noticed that she was near him—' that I envy them, too.'

As the Boy rode down the avenue, he wondered more than once what that speech had meant CHAPTER XI HOW THE BOY RODE IN THE POINT-TO-POINT

Hannah Anne was dressed in her best A cheap hat of many colours perched on her tousled head; a flimsy tan jacket was stretched across her full bosom. Her feet showed in full prominence below her checked skirt, which she never soiled her white cotton gloves by holding up.

It was the day of the Cahirvally Hunt Races, or Point-to-Point. The Ladies' Cup was to be run for, and the Boy, despite all advice, was going to ride Miss Dollie McCarthy's Clear the Way. There were rumours afloat that the lady had asked every man in the county to ride before she had fallen back on the Boy, but he was not proud, and took the mount. Miss Maguire had described the mare as 'a brute with the legs of a hare'; there was some truth in this. If the mare stood up, there was no doubt that she could gallop away from everything in the race, with the exception of Miss Moriarty's horse, The Rover, who was popularly supposed to be a racehorse in disguise.

March was with them. Dry winds licked the moisture, hot suns scorched the earth, black frosts chilled it. The roads were dusty and dry, ringing under the horses' feet with the clanging knell which marks the death of hunting.

Hannah Anne, with her best garments tucked carefully round her, brought in their hot water, and told them, as she came to their several rooms, that 'the missus would herself bring up the breakfasht, for she (Hannah Anne) was away with Tim Carty in his jinnit's cyar to see the races, an' to see Misther Rivers knocking tally out of the whole of thim '—it seemed possible that she saw visions of the Boy riding at full speed over the prostrate bodies of his opponents—' an' the jinnit bein' a thrifle shlow, faith, it was bether for thim to sthart in time.' The hearty blush which accompanied this rambling statement pointed to matrimony in the dim future. But on this being hinted to her, Hannah Anne tossed her head, remarking that, 'faith, ther was more married than kep' good houses, an' the min was apt to change to the divil when once they had ye safe an' sound with the priest's blessin'; an', indade, 'twas only to see thim ridin' that took her out with Tim at all.'

Breakfast was a meal of interludes,

and was brought up by their stern-eyed landlady with running comments to the effect that 'Hannah Anne was out of her head, clane an' dacent, an' that once she heard that Misther Rivers was goin' to ride in the race, all the saints in hivin wouldn't kape her from the races.'

Then Hannah Anne thrust her head for a last glimpse through the doorway. 'Tim's below,' she said, 'waitin' on me. Everything ye want is laid out for ye, and yer ties as white as the dhribbled snow. Indade, I wasn't afther thrustin' that little fool of a man ye have to get out a thing for ye. Look here, now'—this to the Boy—' be afther takin' care of yerself; we'll give the b'ys out there the word, an' they'll be ready to pull down bushes or knock a wall for ye, for I hears from Tim that the baste ye're goin' to ride is apt to be fallin'.'

They put on their pink coats sadly that morning. Memory is a sad equivalent for anticipation. The season was over, the trip to the Promised Land a thing of the past. They had ridden over Nebuchadnezzar's country—where, indeed, he might have taken his fill of grass— for five happy months. They might come back to ride over it again for many years to come. They might lose starts and gain them, cut off angles or get hopelessly left. Bundle along in the ruck which is so hard to get through, or, picking a place close to hounds, slip along with a horse well in hand, the thunder of hoofs behind, and hounds running hard on a breast-high scent in front, over the. perfect country, jumping from springy turf across sound banks and flying walls—all this they might do again, but it would never be quite the same. The strange tongue, the strange people, had grown too familiar. Even Kane-Norton had ceased to rave when his car was arrested in mid-street by gossiping old country-women; had learnt to thread his way with a modicum of patience through a maze of crawling donkey-carts. They could come from the station now, and cleave through a mass of shouting jarveys, and get on the first car with a stoical indifference to the friendly hailing by name which had touched them so much at first.

It would be no surprise when, having ordered their chimney to be swept—to rid the room of puffing smoke—they came in from hunting, weary and wet, to find the room obscured in rolling, choking clouds, and to hear Hannah Anne, after making a spluttering investigation, remark that 'the shweep, the schald to him! had left his brush above in the chimbley whin he wint off'—she could lay hold of the bristles above the fire—' an' now the sorra a chance of gittin' it down till they sent a message to him, an' the Lord sind he might be sober enough to come in the morninV They had also learnt that to pick up unknown horses was to search for pearls among supper oysters.

The banks and walls, the lines of perfect country, the occasional slip over crag and squelch through bog—these would be ever new to them; but the trip in its novelty was over, and—what was to come?

The elder men sat smoking, waiting for the time to start. The Boy, ever restless, had gone down to the club to argue over the merits of every horse in the country.

'Queer thing that we should both be riding the same lady's horses!' Travers said thoughtfully.

It *was* strange. Some impulse had made Miss Maguire ask them to ride her candidates —Bluebeard and Norah—thereby drawing down fresh wrath from Doyle and Moore, who had ridden for her ever since she had grown up, and making the county gossips shake their heads knowingly.

Travers suddenly threw reserve to the wind, and spoke. They must look things in the face, he said; it was no use shying away from them any longer. They were both in love with the same girl—his face said he spoke from his heart; she seemed to like them, but not to favour either. Here Kane-Norton put his glass into his eye. Let it be decided one way or the other. There might be some advantage to the man who spoke first. Travers chewed the cud of thought, and spoke.

'It's an old idea,' he said, 'but it may serve. The lady'—he had almost said

'Sheila'—'says there is nothing between her two horses. Now, let whoever finishes in front of the other tomorrow have the first chance, and no ill-feeling.'

Their hands gripped silently, but their eyes hardened. The two horses, being polished up many miles away might have shivered at the thought of whip and steel if they had heard.

A rattle of wheels, an excited 'Cooey!' from the Boy, announced that it was time to start. Maddigan awaited them, the gray mare pawing freshly.

The cool wind was behind them; wreaths of following dust clung to their tracks. At first the road was empty, but as they passed Lismore it became alive with people, all wending their ways up the winding, narrow road.

The green hillside was dotted with people; two big tents flapped like pinioned birds on the slope. Stalls had sprung up, where one might buy pigs' feet, pipes of gaudy sugar-stick, or huge yellow cakes sprinkled with pink sugar. The Boy expressed a fervent wish to go about gnawing a pig's foot and eating a cake, just to see how long he would survive. They could see the course, a few flags marking the turns. They were to ride to a white house in the distance, turn there, and ride back, keeping one or two flags on their right hands. It was a fair hunting country, banks and walls to jump, and sound turf to gallop over. The tables in the tent were laid ready for luncheon, a goodly array of stout black whisky bottles marking the fact that, whatever happened, there would be something to drink.

Horses were being walked about sheeted. A restless object, with tossing head and tuckeddown tail, represented Clear the Way—overtrained, overgalloped, and consequently irritable. The valley stretched beneath them, straight away to distant Cahirvally, a billowing rise and fall of green, one line of railway intersecting it. A trail of white smoke in the air marked the passage of a train. On one side of the hill lay the green banks, on the other the lighter land, with the stones cropping up through the land, as if the earth had gray measles. But

what fields to ride over when the crag ceased!—light pasture and loose stone walls where, on a scenting day, it was better to pull up a slow horse at once, and not weary him in useless pursuit of the flying pack. At their backs were the purple, heathery hills, the worst bit of the county if a fox refused to come down into the valleys at either side.

The Ladies' Race was first on the card.

Ten starters were marked on it, and the two bookies showed that they were wise men by picking out The Rover for their favourite. Bluebeard, Travers' mount, was next.

The country people babbled of their own fancies. 'Miss Clancy's man is after tellin' me that she has the race widin her pocket.' 'Arrah, man! don't be talking nonsense. Isn't Miss Maguire sure to win? Didn't she take it lasht year, and why not this?' 'Now, lishten to what I'm tellin' ye: Clear the Way 'll be lookin' back for them all if she doesn't knock off the man that's on her.' 'McCarthy's mare, is it, an' she dhrawn up to thrings. What about The Rover? sure, isn't he a racehorse? an' Miss Moriarty she has Timmy Murphy up to ride him.'

The 'brute' Clear the Way was, no doubt, very fast. She was stripped and made ready, and the Boy, with a qualm of nervousness he scorned himself for, dropped into the saddle and gathered up the reins. This the mare acknowledged with a couple of sullen kicks, and moved off with humped back and tuckeddown tail. When he had hunted her, the Boy had been honoured with a severe double bridle; but hunting, apparently, was not racing, and he looked at the big plain snaffle with some dismay She raked at it when he tried to turn her. A winter's hunting had improved the Boy, but he was still far from being a horseman.

As he moved towards the post—or, rather, the field which represented it—he met Sheila Maguire, riding her good gray. Her face was clouded.

'You ought to be ashamed of being on that brute,' she said. This modicum of truth made the Boy flush. 'You en-

danger your own life, and the lives of others. Brute! brute!' She glared at the mare's restless, vicious head. 'Would anything persuade you to get down even now, or at least to try to ride her carefully?'

'To get down—now?' The Boy stared. 'For the rest, as to the "carefully," she is rather self-willed; and—you say I can't ride.'

Shrill across the field came Dollie McCarthy's voice. 'Mr. Rivers! Mr. Riv—ers!' In that moment's importance how she wished that he was a Captain! Swift across the field came the lady herself, a trained skirt in her hand, a plumed hat on her fuzzy head, the general effect tawdry; but she was undoubtedly pretty. Miss Maguire's nose went heavenwards. 'Oh, of course, I see the attraction,' she said icily, and walked away down the field.

They took a canter. The Boy, after receiving some hurried instructions from the fair owner, who whispered them in his ear with due solemnity and caution, found the mare move under him badly; the snaffle was nothing in her wicked mouth, and it was evident that too much oats had disagreed with her.

Then the horses lined up. A hunt race is easy to start. Kane-Norton dropped his hands to Norah's first rush, and, light as a feather, the mare slipped over the bank in front of them; whatever happened, he was sure of a pleasant ride and a safe one. Travers took Bluebeard by the head, sending him along. The old horse was a bit of a slug, but he could gallop and stay for a week.

The thundering hoofs, the sudden rush, drove Clear the Way quite mad. She stuck her lean nose straight out, and cleared the bank from field to field. Absolutely beyond control, she galloped amongst the others, now swerving this way, now that. As they came to the third fence, where they began to bend towards the white house, she caught the bit in her teeth and bolted. The fence the others jumped was an easy one; the mare made for a blind tangle of bough hiding a rotten bank. The country people opened out to let them pass. The Boy heard their shouts, felt a branch graze his cheek, another strike his back, and they were through, flying right out into the country. A better horseman might have succeeded in steadying or turning the mare. The Boy could do neither. The wind rushed to meet him, the earth slipped away beneath the mare's flying feet. Fences loomed up, there was a bound, a slip, and they were over, and all the time, though he did not know it, a wide ravine lay in front of him, a fence to drop in and out of cleverly—a certain fall, and a heavy one, for any horse which tried to fly it. The Boy squeezed in his knees and began to pray that his breath might hold out. As he fled, a gray horse came from the corner of the field and galloped after him rapidly; all eyes were on the racing horses, and after the first moment no one noticed him. No one save the girl on the gray horse, and another figure which detached itself from the crowd and, screaming 'He'll be killed, the darlin' 1' flung itself across the fields, hot on his track.

The Boy sawed, the Boy pulled; the mare kept the bit in her teeth. Her ears were laid back, she wanted to hurt someone; and, unconsciously, his spurs grazed her as she fled. Another bank— she never touched it; then downhill over the next field.

The gray horse cut off an angle and landed close to the mare. The girl riding him took a look at the ravine, which she knew only too well, and then shrieked at the Boy, 'Turn her! Stop her! There's a river in front of you! You/00// you'll be killed if you can't stop!' Fright makes some people irritable.

The Boy understood dimly; he felt that, whatever happened, he must not bear down on the belt of blackthorns in front of him. He pulled one rein, he struck at the mare's head. In answer she swerved wildly, and thundered right into the bank close to her, turning head over heels into the next field with the Boy underneath. Blackness sprang up to meet him; waters roared in his ears; he felt a sharp pain in his arm. Then presently his senses cleared, and he saw Sheila Maguire kneeling beside him, her face very white, and her gray horse grazing close to her. In his confusion he

wondered vaguely whether she had also fallen.

'1 The mare?' he inquired. 'Where is she?'

'Gone. Gone on to—to—the next world, I hope/ said the lady bitterly and with heat. 'Your arm's broken, I believe; your head's cut'—the Boy wiped at a warm stream trickling down his cheek. 'And it's all due to your folly, your obstinacy, your infatuation for that pretty little'

The Boy put out a weak hand. 'Don't jump on a man when he's down,' he said.

'You shall never, as long as you live, ride an awkward horse again,' said Miss Maguire between her teeth.

'Who says so?' asked the Boy. He felt as if he were on an inclined plane and was gradually slipping downwards.

'/ say so,' said the lady tersely; and something salt plashed down her face.

She bent over him, and, though her voice had been harsh, she raised his head very gently;. his face was growing whiter.

Then to them across the fields, her hat gone,. her skirt torn, came a panting, shouting figure. 'Wirra! wirra!'it wailed. 'Is he dead? Didn't he pass me above on the bank for all the world like a sthreak of lightning, an' the horse wid her nose sthuck out like a knife? An' I tellin' him not to be abusin' himself, for the fences this day were med sphecial to knock the quality. Howld on'—this was delivered as she gathered breath to scale the bank—' I have Patsey's bottle of whishky that he bought at the lasht public within in me pocket: 'twill hearten ye.'

These words came on the breeze as Hannah Anne tumbled over the fence with a fresh sound of rending, and landed on all fours by the Boy's side.

'God save ye, Miss Maguire asthore!' she said breathlessly. 'I towld Patsey to come on afther me, but I'm afeared he's waitin' to see the ind of the race. Misther Rivers, what happened to ye at all, at all? Holy Vargin! 'tis a wakeness he has.'

The Boy heard vaguely; he came suddenly to the edge of the incline he had

been on, and slipped over into a dark, still world beneath.

The wind, cool and fresh, shook the thorns in the ravine; the light clouds sped across the blue sky; a sudden hoarse hum of cheering came to them, telling them that the race was at an end—it rose and fell uneven and shrill, but they did not heed, for there in the desolate country were two women weeping over one prostrate self-willed man.

In the meantime the race was going on. Travers and Kane-Norton were sweeping on over the country, riding carefully and well, with due regard to the fences they had to cross. It was an excellent course, but one or two horses came down, and only six of the competitors were well together as they rounded the white farmhouse and turned with their faces towards home. Every fence at the beginning of the race held its fringe of agitated country-folk, who blessed them as they passed. 'Good, begob!' "Tis yeself that can do it!' 'Well over!' 'Timmy Murphy, he has thim all widin his fist; look at the way his bashte is sthalin' over the ground!'

This was strictly true. Miss Maguire's horses were fast, but they were only hunters, and from the first Travers and Kane-Norton recognised the fact that a little long-tailed bay, ridden by a man with a red beard, could slip away from them all when it was asked. Travers was not unchristian as a rule, but there were moments when he breathed something very like a prayer that the bay might—make a mistake. They galloped down to a thatched cottage close to the road, only a few fields from home. Bluebeard was going strong and well, striding easily along, but Travers looked at the long slope before him and felt that the old horse had very little pace in reserve. A red flag, which they had been told to keep to their right, fluttered on the road, and, to his surprise, Travers saw the man on the bay, who was leading, bend away to the left of the house, out of the straight line home. By keeping straight on Travers calculated he would save quite a long piece of ground. He threw aside all idea of the inhabitants being wiser than he was, and taking Bluebeard by the head, he rode him at a low bank into the field by the cottage. Then, as he galloped across a muddy, trampled piece of land, he saw his mistake. To reach the road and leave the flag on his right hand, he must jump a high coped wall out of this uneven, slippery take-off, where cows had been standing all the winter. To go back now would be to lose everything. He looked at the uncompromising gray stones, he looked at the hill above him, and—he kept on. Bluebeard cocked his ears, recognising the task in front of him, dropped back to a trot, and bucked over like a deer. 'Done them!' cried Travers triumphantly. Then came the sound of hoofs close behind, the pant of quick breathing, and—a rattle of falling masonry as Kane-Norton landed beside him. 'Not going to be done, y' know/ remarked that gentleman, 'though I guessed that there was something big down here; but, by Jove! it's a good thing for Norah that the top stone was loose.'

They popped in and out of the road side by side, and swung to the left up the last big field, a huge cheer from the crowd greeting them.

'Here they are!' 'Didn't I know I heard thim passin' below there?' 'The brown has it won!' I tell ye the other has it; he's batin' on now!'

Stride for stride up the field, the horses' necks dark and wet, their muscles rippling, every inch of their bodies strained in answer to their riders' calls on them.

Over the last fence, which was a low fly; then the run-in. Travers, riding Bluebeard hard, slipped ahead; Kane-Norton stole the halflength back. His mare was the speedier, but she was more blown than the old horse. The men's whips were up, the spurs ran red. The people shrieked in frenzied glee: 'Dhrive thim on!' 'Lay in to them!' 'Glory be to the hivins, 'tis a great race entirely!'

The men's teeth were set, their eyes blazed. The wind they made sang to meet them; the mass of people were a

blurred darkness. With a last effort Kane-Norton lifted his mare with knee and bridle, and, with Norah's nose in front, they swam past the judge, who had entered into the excitement and was waving his hands wildly, just as the long-tailed bay came up and slipped into third place, which a few more strides would have made first. Mr. Tim Murphy, a well-known rider, got off disconsolately, and was heard to observe that he 'hoped the divil might sweep Dinny Hickey, that he couldn't have the stones firm on his wall. If the mortar had stuck, one of them would have been left behind, at any rate. I couldn't be beat—only who would have thought of them two facin' Dinny's haggart and jumping out of the cowstand! There was no manner of depindence to be placed on the English, even when they were not in the army.'

Kane-Norton looked round, full of suppressed excitement and triumph. The horses stuck their noses out, their flanks rising and falling like piston-rods as they fought for breath. Never in all their lives had they been given such a gruelling.

'Where's Miss Maguire?' Kane-Norton wedged his eyeglass in and searched for a gray horse. 'She'll be so pleased—her horses first and second.'

'And second,' said Travers sulkily. His heart was bitter within him. It seemed an omen. He had lost the race; he would also lose the lady.

Miss Maguire's groom muttered in subdued tones that 'they had fairly plucked the life out of the horses, an' they havin' the whole way up to sittle it quiet an' dacent; seein' that both horses came from the same stable.'

They weighed. The wind blew cool and sweet, the sun shone—vainly. Where was Miss Maguire, to see her victory? They missed the Boy, but that, considering his mount, was not surprising, and they expected to see him come in at any moment. They made their way through the crowd. Doyle and Moore eyed them sourly; nay, a word bearing a suspicious resemblance to 'fools ' came down the breeze. Tim Murphy, the centre of a sympathizing group, was still

busy with his woes, pointing to the wall below. The booths were crowded with people satisfying their hunger on the strange medley of contents, and babbling of the fine race.

With a peevish gesture, Kane-Norton dimmed his heated glory by putting on his coat. He was buttoning it, when they heard a sudden excited murmur, and saw a crowd coming towards them with something inert in its midst. Also, there at last was the gray horse, and Miss Maguire to hear of her victory. Kane-Norton lunged forward quickly, telling her of his win: 'First and second. Good for your horses, wasn't it?' he said. 'Why, what's this?'

'This' was the Boy's face, white and rather silly, peering over the edge of the patchwork quilt which they had insisted in carrying him in, notwithstanding his assurances that he could walk. He had fainted twice, and they bundled him without much ceremony into the quilt. Hannah Anne, still clutching the bottle of whisky, and abusing Patsey at every step he took, walked by his side.

'Don't be sthirrin' him—don't be sthirrin' himl' she adjured the patient Patsey. ''Tisn't a sack of pytaties ye have, ye goomthawn I Look now, ye shuk him!'—as a faint groan was heard.

Here Patsey remarked, in injured tones, that he'd want to be thramplin' on air, an' not on the land, to be plazin' her; and wouldn't she casht her eye on the others, an' not be blamin' him for iver?'

'You see,' said Miss Maguire, quite ignoring the fact that her horse had won. 'Badly hurt. Fortunately, I—I—happened to be near him when he fell; and this girl ran, too, to help.'

Hannah Anne said 'Praises be!' as she recalled her hurried and tattered flight.

At this moment a shrill voice rose close to them above the hum of the crowd—Miss Dollie McCarthy's staccato tones: 'But where is my mare? She has never come, and no one saw her fall. Where are Clear the Way and Mr. Rivers?'

The gray horse, in answer to a stroke of the whip, clove his way through the crowd, and Miss Maguire confronted the speaker. 'The last I saw of your vicious mare she was going straight to the ravine,' she said. 'If you wish to see Mr. Rivers, he is here.' Her accusing finger pointed to the sheet.

'Dear me!' said Kane-Norton in faint tones. Supposing if ever, in the dim future of matrimony, he should be addressed in that voice!

Dollie McCarthy tossed a tousled head, bit off a sharp retort with difficulty, and made a mournful inspection of the Boy; then she despatched several messengers to look for the absent mare. She walked with them for a few steps, and Patsey, with his head over his shoulder, regaled her with his account of Clear the Way's progress.

'She whipped pasht me like a sthreak of lightnin', out through the bushes, and we thinkin' the eyes was clean torn out of the gintleman. Sure, ye couldn't see the way she was goin', she was that spheedy, and 'twas a mortial pity 'At this point he stumbled, and Hannah Anne cut him short with a box on the ear. Miss McCarthy fell back, watching for her mare. The procession went on, and made its way into a boreen leading across a small patch of bogland to Dunmore.

Travers and Kane-Norton followed, distressed and disappointed. The air seemed to have grown suddenly heavy; the mass of graybrown trees below them, the stretch of country, the blue-gray hills nosing into the blue-gray sky, seemed tinged with a strange melancholy. The wind rustled the coarse yellow grass of the bog, stirring the mystic brown pools, which bore the shimmer of ink in their depths, on the side next to the freshly-cut turf. The old land's sorrows gripped them. Something, they could scarcely have said what, touched their hearts— some dim comprehension of the long struggle which this childish people had made for the toy Liberty, a toy they would scarcely know how to use if it were handed to them. The people who had fought, poured out their blood; perhaps on the very bog they crossed now people could be roused to a semblance of demons with one word,

charmed back to cheery good-heartedness with another, who, left to themselves, lived on from year to year content if their labour brought them enough to eat, who died cheerfully, secure in their religion, with no fear for the future. Trim England fell away as a cloak, and for a moment they seemed to see into the naked hearts of the people they had come amongst. Travers shivered, quickening his steps; it was a relief to reach the wood and catch a glimpse of the garden beyond.

The Boy was speaking weakly at times, and was always instantly repressed by Patsey, who, finding it quite a relief to bully someone else, muttered ' Be aisy' each time. Then he was carried up the stone steps, and sat down in the hall, released at last from the indignity of his parti-coloured quilt; but Hannah Anne, taking advantage of his weakness, arranged it round him like a toga.

Travers and Kane-Norton stood outside.

'He's only shook, not much hurt. And—it's so awkward—for us,' said Kane-Norton slowly. 'For us—how?' asked Travers.

'His being here. Don't you see? Miss Maguire dislikes the Boy so much, it makes it very awkward his being ill here. It may put her out—in many ways. ' Kane-Norton was thinking of the question he meant to ask on the morrow at latest.

'Yes, it's fearfully awkward, and may put her out,' he repeated as he went in.

CHAPTER XII

How Next Year's Hunting Was Arranged For

Kane-norton came down to breakfast at No. 8, Connel Street dressed in his best—a suit of gray tweeds, with the creases of newness striping their legs, a collar which was a pillar of snow among collars, and a tie which it had taken him half an hour to choose. He was visibly nervous in manner, and toyed with the bacon and eggs which reposed in confusion on the big china dish.

Mrs. O'Neill was greatly put out by her handmaiden's prolonged absence,

for Hannah Anne had quite refused to leave the Boy, who was lying at Dunmore. Breakfast that morning was undoubtedly a silent meal. The two men cast furtive glances at each other across the dusty room; they looked sadly at piles of whips and spurs littering the chairs.

It was time to go back to England, and— next year's hunting had to be arranged for. He who once hunts in Cahirvally will always hunt in Cahirvally, if fate will allow him to. They wanted to do more—to live there for at least seven months out of the year.

The window was wide open, the grind of wheels came from the street below, mingling with the blurred Southern accents as a donkey was bidden with a whack to 'Gan out of that!' or a couple of people stopped to argue and gossip. Then high and shrill came the cries of the street-hawkers—dirty women who went round with baskets of dirtier vegetables poised on their heads.

Travers had ordered Maddigan round at an early hour. They possessed an excellent excuse for a morning call: they must go out to see the Boy, who had been left last night with the verdict of ' nothing serious.'

But they knew what was really agitating them—Kane-Norton, by having won the race last night, had also won the right to ask Sheila Maguire first, and Travers, standing by the window, was tortured by misgivings. Norton was undoubtedly handsome, and he possessed in full that certainty of himself which goes so far with some women.

The sky was blue; the breath of spring was in the air. Where would the question be asked? Out in the cool wood, with the hum of its myriad branches as the wind swayed them, the twitter of courting birds, the voices of the spring, waking an answer in the girl's soul? Or in the conservatory, with the heavy scent of flowers, the humid air, the green palms overhead? Travers sighed bitterly, and turned to his friend to tell him that Maddigan, with the ever-ready gray, waited at the door. If he (Travers) could have spoken first, what eloquence he could have used! Kane-

Norton got carefully into a new overcoat. Travers saw with pain that he put away the pipe he usually smoked when driving, and lighted a gold-tipped cigarette. They clattered up the street, bumped over the crossings, and turned into the wide road into the country.

It was a day of cool shadows, of sharp contrasts. The Cahir hills were flecked with gray and with gold. Clouds, as if innumerable sheep had flung their coats off in the heavens, moved across the deep blue of the sky. The distant Mattagh Mountains were chill and blue; their summits, cutting clear across the sky, were snow-tipped, veined like a fair human skin. A cool, sharp wind blew from the east, stirring the hedges where the blackthorn bough starred the tangle of dark boughs, and the tiny green shoots on the may were just beginning to nose out. Maddigan poured gossip into their unwilling ears—of how The Rover yesterday was 'just bought and kep' for the race, the Moriartys bein' in with a lot of racin' people/ and yet how, in his opinion, there was no doubt that, 'if Clear the Way had stood above on her feet, she'd have run him very close in the finish.' But they scarcely heeded or answered him.

The road rang under the gray mare's hoofs as they swung onwards, with the fields, brilliant green now from early grass, stretching all round them.

At last they saw Dunmore in the distance, its woods dark against the sky. They looked again at each other, and a deeper silence fell on them. Certainty was near.

This was fair, but what of next year?

The Boy had insisted on getting up that morning, despite all advice from Hannah Anne, who haunted him until he nearly went crazy. He could not put on his pink, but, unearthing the fact from the butler that he had a new suit which he would be proud to lend, the Boy arrayed himself in it. Then, quite unembarrassed by the knowledge that his feet and arms stretched, very much in the fashion of Mrs. O'Neill's chickens, below the trousers and sleeves, he crawled downstairs, his injured arm in a sling, and a large modicum of sticking-plaster on one side of his face.

There was no one about, and, feeling weaker than he would have cared to own to, he was glad to sit down on the window-seat in the library. The sun shone golden bright outside, lighting up beds of hyacinths and hundreds of daffodils nodding their graceful heads in the cool breeze. Further on a bed of scarlet anemones looked as if the Earth were newly gashed and poured out her blood. There was a distant murmur of lambs' voices, and the muddled, self-sufficient noise of a poultry-yard, where all the feathered tribe seemed bent on making their own voices heard. A turkey-cock sent out vicious rumbling challenges, to be shrieked down by a blatant drake. Then a cock rang an important note, to be drowned.in his turn, as one of his wives wished all the world to know that she—wonderful bird!—had laid an egg. Then all started together again till they merged into a discordant hum.

The Boy listened languidly; his head ached and his arm was painful.

Trouble always presses on her victims when they are weakest; the Boy began to go over his accounts in his mind, and they were not pleasant mental reading. When Ould Tim and the gray were disposed of, it would be time to go off to some clime where a man might make money, even if his powers for office work were nil; or else to sink into genteel poverty at home—pay long visits to rich relations, who plainly looked on you as a nuisance. The Boy sighed wearily; he was not given to the unprofitable art of thinking.

Then Sheila Maguire came into the room. The Boy knew something of ladies' clothes, and he saw that the green blouse she wore showed up her fine skin and fair, abundant hair. She stood looking at him.

'Well?' she said.

'Well,' said the Boy lamely.

He felt the awkwardness of his position.

'I hope you're better this morning,' she went on.

'Oh yes, thank you.' It came to him suddenly, bringing the blood to his cheeks, that he was a visitor in the house of a girl who particularly disliked him, and his immediate anxiety was to get away. 'I'm really all right. I could get up quite easily. If I had not been dazed, I should have gone away last night. I'm most awfully sorry to put you out, and —I'm sure they'll come for me as early as possible,' he said stiffly.

A shadow fell on the girl's face. The fresh tints died out of her skin.

'You—you are very anxious to get away, then?' she asked quietly.

He was conscious of having been perhaps uncourteous.

'Yes, anxious—as I'm sure you are to be rid of me. And, besides, I've really a lot to do at the lodgings. We move off in a day or two, a week at furthest for me. I have to get back.'

Sheila Maguire stood quite still her hand on the curtain. The Boy looked with embarrassed blue eyes into her gray ones, and a thrill of unknown, almost unrecognised feeling shot through his frame. His voice, when he spoke, was in consequence stiffer than before.

1 You've been more than good,' he said. 'I don't know *why* you came after me yesterday.'

'Came after you!' Rimmel himself would not have been ashamed of the colour which mantled the girl's cheeks. 'I assure you, I never came after you— never! I saw you running away, and as the race was running, and I was riding, and you were—falling—you see, I—I'

The Boy intimated gravely that it sounded a little like poetry, but he was sure that he understood perfectly, and that it must indeed have been pure accident which had brought her to *his* aid.

Strange to say, she looked dissatisfied at this reading of her meaning, which she had been at such pains to make him see.

Silence fell on them. The self-sufficient voices of the poultry-yard, the bleating of the lambs, became again apparent. Then a yell, and the squawking of many frightened ducks cut across the silence. There was the sound of scurrying, and an old woman in pursuit of a brown terrier rushed across the grass. 'Chasin' the dooks, are ye? May the divil mind ye! Ye expect thim to lay eggs, ye schamer, an' ye whippin' iviry feather out of their tails!' The dog vanished into the trees, the woman after him, her shouts growing fainter in the distance.

'My terrier. He is so fond of chasing ducks,' said Sheila apologetically. 'And Biddy never gets used to him. She will come back presently to scold me. I am not, in her eyes, grown up as yet.'

'An English henwife would give warning. This old lady loses hours of her time in futile chasing, and then in all probability feeds that dog on milk when the evening comes. Bless them! I love them all,' said the Boy wistfully.

'And yet you are going away, and will never be here again.'

'Because I can't help it The others can make arrangements for next year. Mine will be made for me by an empty-handed Fate.'

'1 wonder,' said Miss Maguire softly, 'I wonder!'

There was a clatter somewhere in the house, followed by raised voices arguing.

'It's only Hannah Anne,' explained Sheila, smiling. 'She is making you some concoction of egg-and-whisky, and has taken the whole household, including the cook, into her service for the time being.'

The Boy remarked that he hoped Miss Maguire was prepared to buy some new china. The Boy could never tune his tongue to conventional politeness.

'And yet—you are leaving it all,' said the girl again.

The tendrils of the land which had fastened round the Boy's heart stirred, hurting him. His thoughts flew again to the hillside where Martin and Norah lived. The gorse-bushes were growing golden now; the bog below was sending its fresh breath across the desolate land. He looked up at the girl standing by him, and he, Norman Rivers, the scoffer at all sentiment, became suddenly aware of a fact which made him more anxious than ever to get out of the house, to get away anywhere, so that no one might ever know of the sudden thought which

had come to him.

Sheila Maguire came closer to him.

'Supposing,' she said—her voice was tremulous—'supposing—I want to ask your advice —that—that you, I, any-one—had it in our power to offer some-one else—everything that could make that person happy, and yet that it was not that someone's place to offer, and they felt sure the—other person— would never ask— for him—for them-selves.'

'I'm afraid I scarcely understand,' said the Boy weakly. Was she asking his advice about the other two? he wondered.

'And one knew that the other person would never ask, yet he—they—were the kind of person who would be sure to give a truthful answer,' she repeated with insistence.

The Boy stared at the avenue. Why did they not come to fetch him? He knew now why he had quarrelled so much with the tall girl close to him. He knew that deep in his boyish, care-less heart he had fallen in love with her. His head whirled, and he was ashamed. Even if he thought she liked him, how could he, a pauper, ever say anything to the heiress of Duntnore? And now she was, so far as he could gather, actually asking his advice about his two friends, though why she should think they would not have sufficient courage to ask her to marry he could not imagine.

'They're both simply dying to ask you,' he said bluntly; 'any fool could see that.'

'Some fools can't see anything,' said the girl sharply, her cheeks crimson again.

Then breathlessly, her voice indistinct, for her face was half hidden in the window-curtain, she went on speaking:

'If I found you—a situation—which would mean your staying here—always, would you —take it?'

The Boy looked out across the flower-beds, looked on to the land he loved. Then he laughed a little bitterly.

'A situation! As what? Groom, or headtrainer, or steward, or poacher?' he asked impatiently.

'It has one drawback. It would in-clude— you would have to marry to take it.'

'I—have to marry!' said the Boy in staccato tones. How his head ached, and this was silly!' Who am I to marry?'

'I thought — of—myself.' She flung the words from behind the window-cur-tain as if they had been stones. 'There I I had to ask you. Now say no. *You* won't hesitate.'

'Heavenly powers!' said the Boy, falling back on Hannah Anne's vocabu-lary in his excitement and astonishment. 'You—and you never liked me. You al-ways quarrelled with me—and the oth-ers are sure'

'Oh, you're quite an owl!' said the girl, putting her hands up to hide her crimson cheeks.

At this point the Boy recovered him-self, and remarked that he didn't intend to be called names. Also, with his unin-jured arm, he made Sheila uncover her face in a way which showed that, if he were to be man, he also meant to be master.

'You haven't said—no,' muttered the girl feebly.

Incoherently the Boy explained his poverty, his absolute unsuitability for the position of husband or anything else. But there was a new note in his voice.

'And—because I am rich am I never to be happy?' muttered Sheila in muf-fled tones. 'I' know I felt that, if you didn't care, you are honest enough to say so, and not think of hurting my feel-ings.'

'It would be far unkinder to marry a woman one did not care for than to tell her so straight out,' said the Boy. 'I—great Scott!—I suppose you knew I cared long ago, though I didn't myself.'

'You were *not* born for a courtier,' said the girl, smiling contentedly.

'But what I want to know is, when did you think of caring for a brainless duffer like me?' The Boy felt a strange tide of happiness creeping over him. He knew now what had spoken to him, why his thoughts had flown so often to the lovers he had helped.

'I suppose I liked you from the first,'

she answered. 'But when I knew first that there was—no one else—I think it was the evening when you threw me into the hay in a bundle. I have always bullied everyone; it was quite a change to be bullied. Think—I was jealous yesterday of that Dollie girl! I—of ktrf

The Boy hoped that she might not get tired of it, but something in the face turned towards him said that she would find it very hard to get tired of him in any way.

'But, I say—the others?' said the Boy after an interlude. He was trying to get used to his position.

'They—merely wished to hunt at Cahirvally,' said Sheila dryly.

'Not Travers; he's fond of you. I'm not so sure about Kane-Norton. He likes that Martin girl.'

At this point Sheila Maguire remarked that he would never lose anything by not telling the truth.

Old Biddy, the fowl-woman, came panting back across the grass, and, seeing Miss Maguire, stopped to tell her daily tale of woe—of how Trust had 'set on thim ducks, an' what was the good of wastin' good yellow male on thim, whin they was run to fiddle-sthrings iviry minute an' hour of the day?' She went on, grumbling and waving her stick.

The Boy looked again out of the window. Cahirvally, with its sunny slopes, its rim of hills—Cahirvally was his for the future. He could chase foxes, shoot birds, kill fish, by field and river, bog and wood. And there was something even better. He drew a long breath of pure thankfulness, and laid his aching head on the girl's cool hand.

The door was banged open. There was a clatter of glass, and Hannah Anne burst into the room, bearing a tray laden with two steaming glasses of egg-flip and a decanter of brandy.

'A tashte of an egg,' she said, 'to hearten ye. Not a sowl would I let touch barrin' meself, an' the cook below dyin' to be at it. An' I brought the spherrits, too, from the man, in case 'tisn't sthrong, for I put no more than two glasses in it.'

'Hannah,' said Sheila, taking the boy's hand, 'will you come and be our

housemaid?'

'Yer, yer Glory to the hivins this night!'

The tray dropped with a flopping crash; the brandy, the beaten egg, flowed in a smoking, smelling stream across the carpet. The glasses were splintered ruins.

'Glory be, blessin's!' said Hannah, utterly oblivious. 'Darlin' to ye, sir, but ye'll be the fine couple, an' proud I'll be to serve with ye! Though how '—she grew thoughtful—' how the miss-us 'll iver find another to be so careful I'm not rightly afther knowin'; but, sure, one can't have everything.'

She trod the glasses under her feet as she rushed across to wring their hands.

Travers and Kane-Norton were coming up the avenue, when they espied Miss Maguire and the Boy just coming out of the French window. The Boy walked slowly, and was supported by the lady's arm.

They got off the car, and walked to the house across through the flower-beds.

'Travers,' said Kane-Norton suddenly, ' I'm not conceited, but I think—she likes me.'

He felt it would be only kind to let Travers know now there was no object in his going on hoping.

'Possibly,' said Travers sourly.

With possession in his eye, Kane-Norton eyed the square house, the gray wall of the garden, the range of stabling, the lawn dotted with stately old trees.

'I should fence off the avenue," he said to himself, following his thoughts.

The Boy and Miss Maguire stood at the window, a raw reek of brandy coming past them to the outer air. Hannah Anne had now gathered the broken glass into her apron, and, being alone, was mopping up the wet with a table-cloth.

The Boy responded to their inquiries. He listened, smiling, as they apologized profusely for the trouble he had given.

'The Boy ought never to have ridden the brute,' said Kane-Norton; 'he should stick to trained horses. Now, next year'

'Ah! Then, you've already made your

arrangements for next year?' said Sheila.

'Arrangements!' When they remembered how nebulous the arrangements were, and how much they depended on her, they stared at each other and flushed, and the flush was not lost on Sheila.

'My arrangements,' said the Boy mischievously, 'are made for next year. I am taking a situation here.'

'A—what?' said Travers.

'Yes, as steward. Isn't that it?' He looked up at the blushing girl. 'Sheila wants someone—especially to keep out poachers; but she won't take an unmarried man, so she's going to marry me herself to settle it.'

The men stared blankly. The solid ground seemed to slide away beneath their feet. The Boy! The Boy, whom the lady had always disliked, who on his part had never even been civil to her—the Boy was to gain the coveted prize! The babble of the spring outside cut across the stillness.

Then Kane-Norton's eyeglass flew to the full length of its string, and the humour of it struck Travers, so that he smiled—the saddest smile he had ever smiled in his life.

'You haven't congratulated us,' said the Boy possessively.

'Believe me, with all my heart I shall always wish for your happiness,' said Travers quietly, and his face was the first blot on the fair page of the Boy's new life.

Hannah Anne burst through the window, the table-cover, heavy with the fumes of brandy, in her hand.

'The blessin's of hivin be about thim!' she said. Clearly she had been listening. 'Amn't I comin' to mind the house for thim, an' the missus within 'll be leppin' out of her skhin to lose me."

She gave a final wave to the brandied cloth, shook the chinking glass in her apron, and vanished to 'whip another brace of eggs' for the Boy.

'1 imagine,' said Sheila, 'that, if we wish to keep anything intact in the house, it might possibly be wiser to marry Hannah to Patsey as speedily as possible.'

'So next year is settled for,' said the Boy dreamily. His head was still aching sadly.

'Yes. Won't you come to stay with us? Cahirvally hunting will be worth it,' said Sheila hospitably, but with a twinkle in her eye. She was quick to note the spotlessness of Kane-Norton's attire, the present blankness of his expression.

'Marry—the Boy,' said Kane-Norton. 'The Boy!'

He stood where he had first heard the news. Then he slowly rescued his eyeglass, and as he did so a memory of velvety, worshipping eyes rose to bring him comfort. It was possible that Kane-Norton might also marry.

There was bitterness in the men's hearts as they recalled their conversations, their certainty that one or other would win the prize. And now—to come to stay with the Boy!

But they looked at the country; they saw through the gap in the trees the billowing country all round. They became composed, offered many congratulations, and accepted the invitation.

The arrangements for next year's hunting were completed.

Lightning Source UK Ltd.
Milton Keynes UK
UKOW06f1927040914

238111UK00010B/557/P